Dwayne's Guitar Lessons Presents:

Beginner's Guide to Acoustic Guitar Mastery

From Novice to Professional

By
Guitar Teacher
Dwayne Jenkins

Introduction

Welcome to your journey into the world of acoustic guitar playing! Whether you're a complete beginner or someone with a bit of experience, this guide is designed to help you develop the skills and knowledge needed to become a proficient guitarist.

The acoustic guitar is a versatile and expressive instrument that can bring joy and creativity to your life. Through these lessons, you'll explore the fundamental techniques and concepts that will serve as the foundation for your musical adventure.

The acoustic guitar is renowned for its rich, resonant tones and its ability to convey a wide range of musical emotions. From the gentle melodies of folk music to the intricate fingerpicking styles of classical guitar, this instrument opens up a world of musical possibilities.

Learning to play the acoustic guitar is not just about mastering techniques; it's about finding your voice and expressing yourself through music. As you embark on this journey, you'll discover the unique sound that you can create with each strum and pluck of the strings.

Throughout this guide, we've structured the content to build your skills progressively. We'll start with the basics, such as understanding the parts of your guitar and how to tune it, before moving on to more advanced topics.

Each chapter is designed to be engaging and informative, with practical exercises and quizzes to reinforce your learning. By the end of this guide, you'll have a solid foundation and the confidence to explore more complex techniques and styles.

As you progress, you'll delve into topics such as arpeggios, fingerstyle, and music theory. Each chapter builds on the previous ones, ensuring a comprehensive learning experience.

Remember, learning the guitar is a journey, not a destination. It's important to be patient with yourself and enjoy the process of discovery and growth.

Regular practice, coupled with a genuine passion for music, will lead to continuous improvement and personal satisfaction. So, pick up your guitar, open your mind to the endless possibilities, and let your musical journey begin!

Sincerely, Dwayne Jenkins

Table of Contents

Chapter I: Understanding Your Instrument

Lesson 1: Parts of the Guitar

Understanding the various parts of your acoustic guitar is essential for every beginner. Familiarity with these components will not only help you communicate more effectively with other musicians and instructors but also assist you in maintaining and caring for your instrument.

The Body and Neck

- **Body:** The body is the largest part of the guitar and is responsible for producing sound. It consists of the top (soundboard), back, and sides.

The soundboard is crucial as it amplifies the vibration of the strings and produces the beautiful sound of the instrument.

- **Neck:** The neck is the long, slender part of the guitar that connects the body to the headstock. It houses the fretboard (or fingerboard), where you press down the strings to create different notes.

The neck is typically made of wood and may include a truss rod to adjust its curvature.

Strings and Frets

- **Strings:** Most acoustic guitars have six strings made of either steel or nylon. Each string is tuned to a specific pitch, and its vibration produces sound.

Learning how to identify and tune each string is fundamental to making the instrument sound pleasant to the ear.

- **Frets:** Frets are the metal strips embedded along the fretboard. They divide the neck into fixed segments, allowing you to play different notes by pressing the strings down at various positions.

By knowing these basic parts of your guitar, you will lay the groundwork for further study and practice. Look at the picture below to familiarize yourself with other basic parts of the guitar.

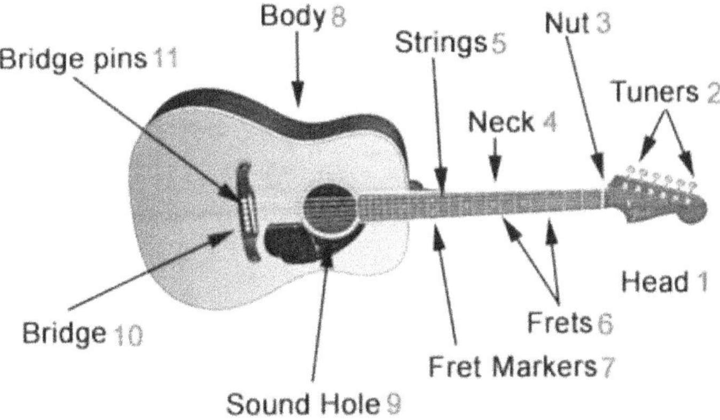

Lesson 2: Tuning the Guitar

Tuning your guitar is a crucial skill for any aspiring guitarist. Proper tuning ensures that your instrument sounds its best and that you can play along with other musicians or recordings accurately.

There are several methods to tune your guitar, and understanding each will help you find what works best for you.

Standard Tuning

The most common tuning for an acoustic guitar is standard tuning. In standard tuning, the strings are tuned to the notes E, A, D, G, B, and E, from the thickest string (6th string) to the thinnest string (1st string). Memorizing this sequence is essential as it forms the basis of many other tunings.

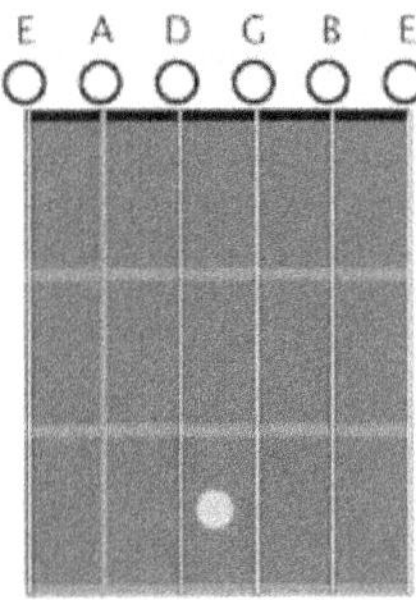

Using a Tuner vs. Tuning by Ear

- **Using a Tuner:** Electronic tuners are practical and precise tools for ensuring your guitar is in tune. They often come in clip-on, pedal, or app form and can automatically detect the pitch of each string.

Using a tuner is especially helpful for beginners as it provides instant feedback, a large display for seeing the pitch, and is easy to use.

- **Tuning by Ear:** Developing this skill is beneficial for any musician. This method involves comparing the pitch of each string to a reference note or another string.

You can use a piano, another guitar, or a tuning fork as your reference. Tuning by ear helps enhance your pitch recognition and musicality over time.

Tips for Effective Tuning

1. **Tune Regularly:** Make it a habit to check your tuning before every time you play. Changes in temperature and humidity can affect your guitar's tuning stability.
2. **Stretch the Strings:** Gently stretching new strings can help them stay in tune longer. When putting them on, slightly stretch them as you do so; this will help prevent them from breaking when tuning them to pitch.
3. **Tune Upwards**: Always tune from a lower pitch upwards to the correct note. This method ensures that the string tension is consistent, reducing the chances of slipping out of tune.

By mastering the art of tuning, you'll ensure that your guitar always sounds its best, making your practice sessions more enjoyable and productive. As you become more comfortable with tuning, you'll be able to explore alternative tunings and expand your musical repertoire.

Lesson 3: Holding the Guitar

Properly holding the guitar is essential for comfortable and effective playing. Whether sitting or standing, how you hold your guitar can significantly impact your playing and help prevent strain or injury.

Let's explore the two main positions for holding your guitar and some tips to improve your technique.

Sitting Position

When sitting, it's important to find a balance between comfort and support. Follow these steps to hold your guitar correctly while seated:

- **Choose the Right Chair**: Avoid chairs with armrests, as they can interfere with your playing.

Your feet should be flat on the ground, and your knees should be at a 90-degree angle. Of course, everyone is a little bit different in height and weight, so it's best to make adjustments when needed.

- **Angle the Neck:** Tilt the neck of the guitar slightly upwards. This angle makes it easier to access the fretboard and reduces wrist strain.

Your objective is to reach the entire fretboard with ease for playing chords and single notes.

- **Maintain Good Posture**: Keep your back straight and shoulders relaxed. Avoid hunching over the guitar to prevent tension and discomfort.

The main thing is that you are comfortable when the guitar is resting in your lap. You can easily reach all six strings on the body, and you can reach the whole fretboard. This will give you the best learning experience and your best chance for success.

- **String Changes**: Regularly changing your strings can improve your guitar's sound and playability. Old strings can become dull and challenging to play. Change strings every few months when you notice a decline in sound quality.

- **Cleaning Your Guitar**: Use a soft cloth to wipe down your guitar after playing to remove sweat and oils that can damage the finish. Occasionally, use a guitar-specific cleaner and polish to maintain the wood's condition.

- **Neck and Action Adjustments**: The neck's curvature, also known as the relief, is designed to provide clearance for string vibration. If this is out of sync, it can affect playability.

If you notice fret buzz or have difficulty playing the strings, consider adjusting the truss rod or bridge. It's often best to consult a professional to handle these adjustments,

Pickup Maintenance: Keep pickups free of dust and debris. If you're experiencing sound issues, checking the pickup height or connections may be necessary.

You can easily make these adjustments to suit your playing style.

By regularly tuning and maintaining your guitar, you'll ensure it remains in excellent condition and provides you with the best possible playing experience. With these foundations in place, you're ready to dive deeper into your musical journey.

Chapter I Quiz

In Chapter 1, we covered the basics. These are what will develop your foundation and allow all your other lessons to stand on.

Q: Which part is responsible for amplifying the string vibration?
A: ____

Q: What is the purpose of the fretboard on the guitar?
A: ____

Q: What is the sixth string tuned to in standard tuning?
A: ____

Q: How is using an electronic tuner better than tuning by ear?
A: ____

Q: How should the guitar be positioned while sitting playing it?
A: ____

Q: What is the key benefit of using a guitar strap?
A: ____

Chapter I Summary

First, you learn about parts of the guitar. The body, the neck, the fretboard, and so forth. Helping you to communicate more effectively with other musicians and assisting you in maintaining and caring for your instrument.

Second, you learn about one of the most important things to know: tuning your guitar. A critical skill to master. Proper tuning ensures your guitar sounds its best, and you can play along with others accurately.

Third, you learn how to hold the guitar properly, which is essential for comfortable and effective playing. Whether you're sitting or standing, the way you hold your guitar can significantly affect your playing ability and prevent strain or injury.

Fourth, you learn about some basic guitar maintenance. This will increase your knowledge and appreciation for the finely crafted instrument.

Lastly, these first few lessons will provide a solid foundation. This will give the rest of this training and others you will learn in the future a place to stand on. Enhancing your musicianship more proficiently.

Chapter II: Getting Comfortable

Lesson 4: Playing Positions

Finding the right playing position is crucial for effective guitar practice and performance. Your posture and how you hold your guitar can affect your comfort, technique, and even the sound you produce. Let's explore some common playing positions and tips to help you find what works best for you.

Classical Position

The classical position is often recommended for beginners as it promotes good posture and allows for optimal finger movement across the fretboard. Follow these steps to adopt the classical position:

1. **Use a Footstool**: Place your left foot on a footstool to raise your left leg slightly. This elevation helps position the guitar properly.

- **Position the Guitar:** Rest the guitar on your left thigh if you're right-handed (or right thigh if you're left-handed). The guitar's body should rest against your chest, with the neck angled upwards.

- **Maintain Alignment:** Keep your back straight and both shoulders relaxed. Your left hand should be free to move along the fretboard without strain.

As I said before, the main goal is to be comfortable as you play the guitar. Be able to reach all parts of the body and neck.

- **Ensure Balance:** The guitar should feel balanced without requiring excessive gripping or tension. It should easily rest on your leg even if your hands are not on it. This will let you relax while playing.

Casual Position

The casual position is more relaxed and often used outside of formal settings. It can be more comfortable for casual playing and performances:

- **Place the Guitar on Your Right Thigh:** If you're right-handed, rest the guitar on your right thigh (or left thigh if you're left-handed). The guitar should rest naturally against your body.

- **Keep the Neck Parallel:** The neck of the guitar should remain relatively parallel to the ground, allowing easy access to all frets.

By experimenting with these positions and finding what feels best for you, you'll enhance your comfort and efficiency while playing the guitar.

- **Relax Your Body**: Ensure your shoulders, arms, and hands are relaxed. Avoid hunching over the guitar to prevent tension and discomfort.

- **Monitor Your Wrist Position**: Keep your wrist straight and flexible to facilitate smooth transitions between chords and notes.

Tips for Finding Your Ideal Position

- **Experiment**: Try both positions to see which feels more natural and comfortable for you.

By approaching the guitar this way, you will discover what works best for you and your playing style.

- **Use a Mirror**: Practice in front of a mirror to observe your posture and make necessary adjustments.

Allowing you to see yourself from a different perspective. A very common way to make improvements.

- **Listen to Your Body**: Notice any signs of discomfort or strain, and adjust your position accordingly.

You should never feel strain when holding the guitar. You should always feel comfortable and relaxed. If not, make adjustments to make this happen.

By experimenting with these positions and finding what feels best for you, you'll enhance your comfort and efficiency while playing.

Lesson 5: Reading Charts and Tabs

Reading music is an essential skill for any guitarist, and understanding how to read chord charts and guitar tabs will greatly enhance your ability to learn new songs and communicate with other musicians. Let's explore these tools and how you can use them effectively.

Understanding Chord Charts

Chord charts are diagrams that show you how to play chords on the guitar. They are straightforward and quick to learn, making them an invaluable resource for any beginner.

- **Diagram Layout:** A chord chart resembles the neck of a guitar, with vertical lines representing the strings and horizontal lines representing the frets.

- **Finger Placement:** Dots on the grid indicate where to place your fingers. Numbers inside the dots correspond to the fingers you should use: 1 for the index, 2 for the middle, 3 for the ring, and 4 for the pinky.

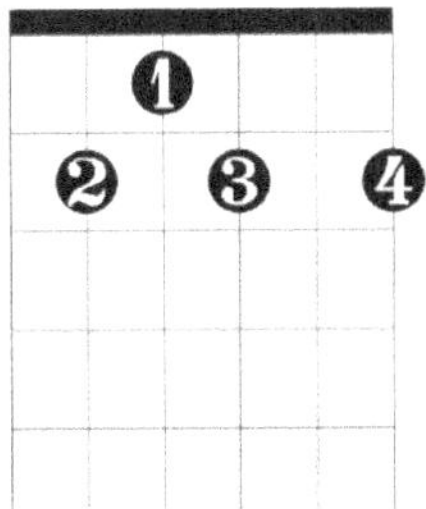

The B7 chord chart.

- **Chord Variations:** Chord charts often show different variations of the same chord, allowing you to choose the version that best suits your playing style or the song's requirements.

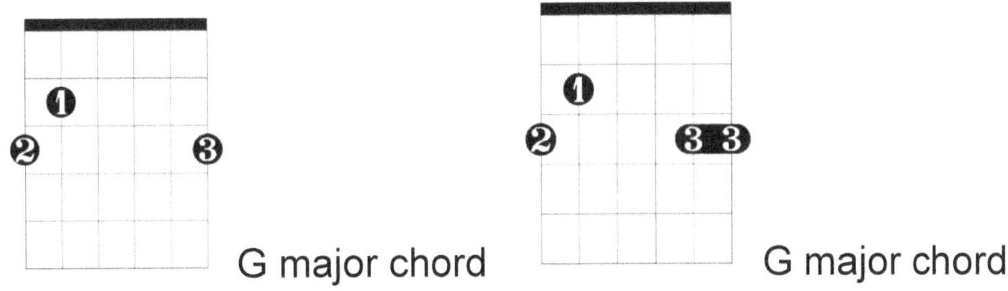

G major chord   G major chord

Notice how these two chords are similar, but slightly different.

- **Practice Tip:** Start by familiarizing yourself with basic open chords such as C, G, D, and E minor. Practice moving between these chords to develop smooth transitions.

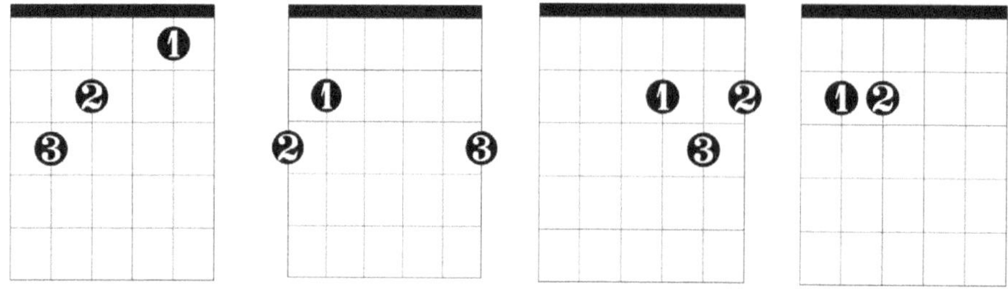

Understanding Guitar Tabs

Guitar tabs, or tablature, provide a detailed representation of how to play melodies, solos, and riffs. Unlike traditional sheet music, tabs are specifically designed for stringed instruments. Here's how to read them:

- **The Layout:** Tabs consist of six horizontal lines, each representing a guitar string. The bottom line corresponds to the low E string, and the top line represents the high E string.

- **Dots and Numbers:** Dots on the chart indicate where to place your fingers, and numbers may indicate which finger to use (1 for index, 2 for middle, 3 for ring, and 4 for pinky).

Not all chord charts will indicate which fingers, but they will all indicate their placement.

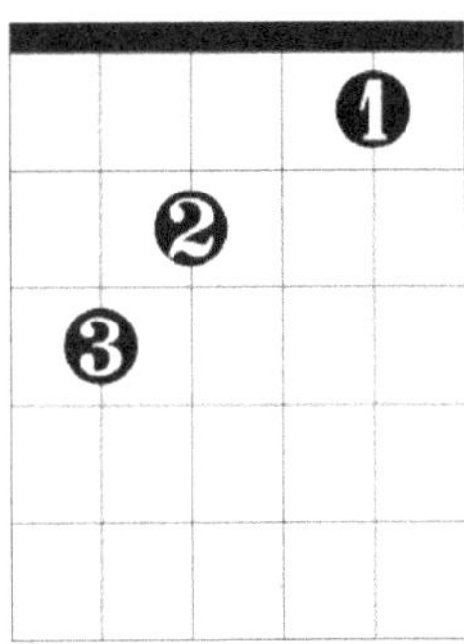

Here is an example of a C major chord chart. The numbers indicate what fingers you use and where you place them. Remember, with chord charts, the guitar is facing upward.

The low E string is on the left, and the chart will feature the first five frets. If the frets go past the first five, there will be a number outside the chord chart on the left to indicate this.

Deciphering Guitar Tabs

Guitar tablature, or tabs, is a form of musical notation indicating instrument fingering rather than musical pitches. Tabs are particularly popular for guitar music.

- **Tab Layout**: Tabs consist of six lines that represent the six strings of the guitar. The top line is the high E string, and the bottom line is the low E string.

- **Numbers**: Numbers on the lines indicate which fret to press on a particular string. For instance, a "5" on the 5th line means you press the fifth fret of the A string.

- **Reading Left to Right**: Tabs are read from left to right, much like reading a book, which dictates the sequence of notes to be played.

This is what differentiates them from chord charts. Which are read like the guitar is facing upward. You'll also need to remember, that when reading guitar tabs, the strings are upside down.

- **Special Symbols**: Tabs often include symbols for techniques such as bends, slides, hammer-ons, pull-offs, and others, helping you to understand the nuances of playing the music.

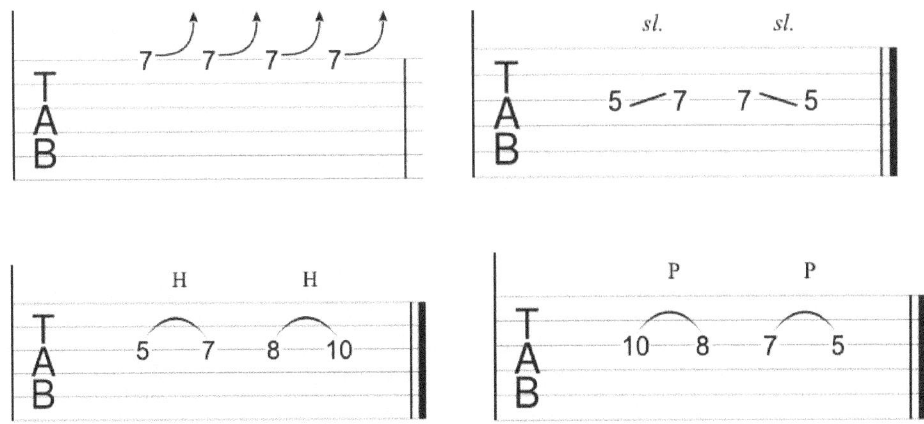

When it comes to playing melody, being able to read these types of symbols will come in very handy.

Tips for Mastering Charts and Tabs

- **Start Simple:** Begin with simple chord charts and tabs to build your confidence.

- **Practice Regularly**: Incorporate reading charts and tabs into your daily practice routine to improve your skills.

- **Listen and Play**: Whenever possible, listen to the song you're learning while following along with the chart or tab to understand the timing and feel.

- **Seek Guidance**: If you're struggling, don't hesitate to ask a teacher or a more experienced guitarist for help.

By learning to read chord charts and guitar tabs, you'll expand your ability to learn new music and communicate effectively with other musicians. This skill opens up a world of musical possibilities, allowing you to explore different styles and genres with ease.

Lesson 6: Common Chords

Learning common chords is a fundamental step in your guitar journey, as these chords form the basis of many songs. By mastering them, you'll be able to play a wide variety of music and gain confidence in your playing abilities.

Essential Chords for Beginners

- **Open Chords:**

Open chords are played using open strings, making them easier for beginners. Some of the most common open chords include:

> **C Major (C):** A bright-sounding chord that is foundational in many songs.

> **G Major (G):** Known for its full, resonant sound, G Major is a staple in many genres.

> **D Major (D):** A lively chord that is often used in folk and country music.

E Minor (Em): A simple yet versatile chord that evokes a somber mood.

A Minor (Am): Offers a melancholic sound often used in ballads and blues.

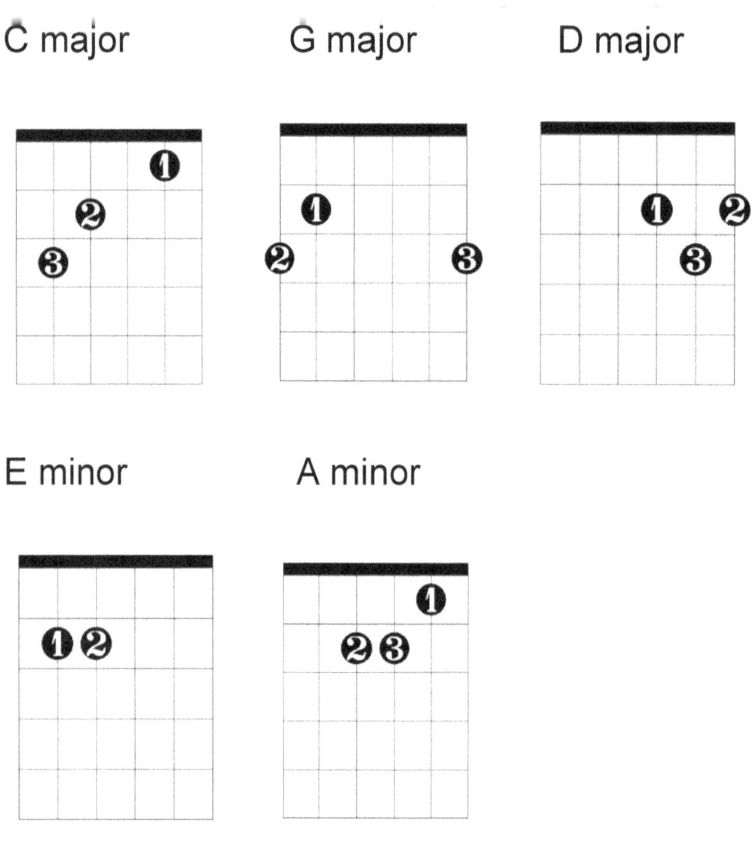

C major G major D major

E minor A minor

These are your five basic guitar chords to start out with. These are found in hundreds of songs and will make up the foundation of your guitar chord vocabulary.

- **Barre Chords:**

Once comfortable with open chords, you can move on to barre chords, which allow you to play shapes up and down the neck. The most common barre chord shapes are:

F Major (F): Often the first barre chord learned, requiring you to use your index finger to press down all strings across a fret.

B Minor (Bm): A minor chord that uses the same barre technique as F Major.

F major bar chord   B minor bar chord

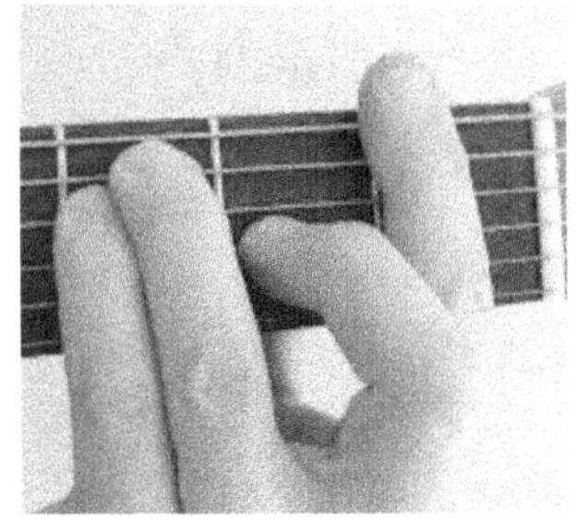

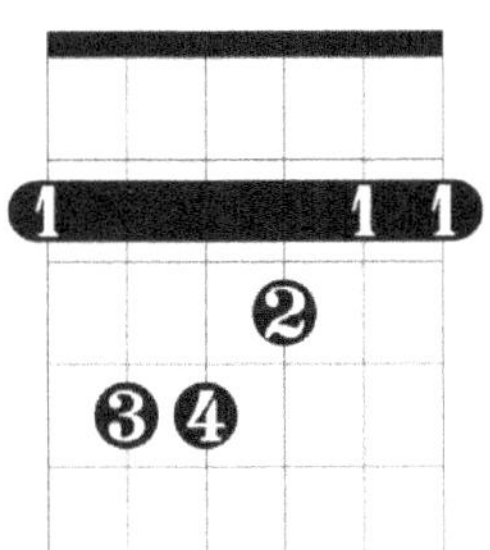

This is an F# bar chord chart. Notice the bar.

Tips for Practicing Chords

- **Finger Positioning:** Ensure your fingers are pressing down on the strings just behind the frets to produce a clean sound.

Avoid touching adjacent strings to prevent muting them. You will also need to play open chords with your fingertips.

- **Smooth Transitions:** Practice moving between chords slowly at first, focusing on smooth transitions. Gradually increase your speed as you become more comfortable.

Start out by switching between two chords at a time. Many great songs are made up of only three chords.

- **Consistent Practice:** Dedicate time each day to practicing chords. Repetition will help build muscle memory, making chord changes more natural.

By mastering these common chords, you will build a solid foundation. As you become more confident, you'll be able to tackle a wider range of songs and explore new musical styles.

Chapter II Quiz

In Chapter 2, you have learned about playing positions, reading chord charts, guitar tabs, and playing common chords. All are critical to the foundation of your development.

Q: What is the primary advantage of using a footstool?

A: ____

Q: Where should the neck be in a casual playing position?

A: ____

Q: What do the vertical lines in chord charts represent?

A: ____

Q: What do the numbers mean when reading guitar tabs?

A: ____

Q: What are the five most common open chords?

A: ____

Q: How do barre chords benefit differently from open chords?

A: ____

Chapter II Summary

<u>First</u>, you learn about the importance of proper playing position for effective practice and performance. Your posture and how you hold your guitar can affect your comfort, technique, and the sound quality you produce when playing.

<u>Second</u>, make sure you fully understand the notes of the musical alphabet, sharps and flats, chords, and major and minor scales. These will provide the foundation for understanding songs and crafting your own compositions.

<u>Third</u>, learn to read chord charts and guitar tabs. These tools provide a visual representation of music, allowing you to gain insight into songs and their components. This will enable you to explore more complex musical landscapes.

<u>Fourth</u>, develop rhythm and timing. This is crucial for any guitarist. This forms the backbone of most songs and provides a solid foundation and understanding of the basics of music.

<u>Lastly</u>, by developing a strong sense of rhythm and timing, you will be able to play and craft music with greater confidence. Allowing you to improve your musicianship and set a solid foundation for future lessons to come.

Chapter III: Strumming and Rhythm

Lesson 7: Basic Strumming Patterns

Strumming is an essential technique for any guitarist, as it forms the rhythmic backbone of many songs. By mastering a variety of strumming patterns, you'll be able to add depth and texture to your playing, making your music more engaging and dynamic.

Downstrokes and Upstrokes

Understanding the basic components of strumming downstrokes and upstrokes is crucial. These are the building blocks of all strumming patterns:

- **Downstrokes:** Strum downward across the strings, typically starting from the thicker strings and moving towards the thinner ones.

This motion often emphasizes the beat, creating a strong, steady rhythm.

- **Upstrokes.** Strum upward, usually starting from the thinner strings and moving towards the thicker ones.

Upstrokes are generally lighter and used to create a sense of lift or syncopation in your playing.

Basic Strumming Patterns

Here are a few simple strumming patterns to get you started. Practice these patterns slowly at first, gradually increasing your speed as you become more comfortable.

- **Down-Down-Down-Down:** A straightforward pattern where you strum down on each beat. This is great for beginners and helps to establish a consistent rhythm.

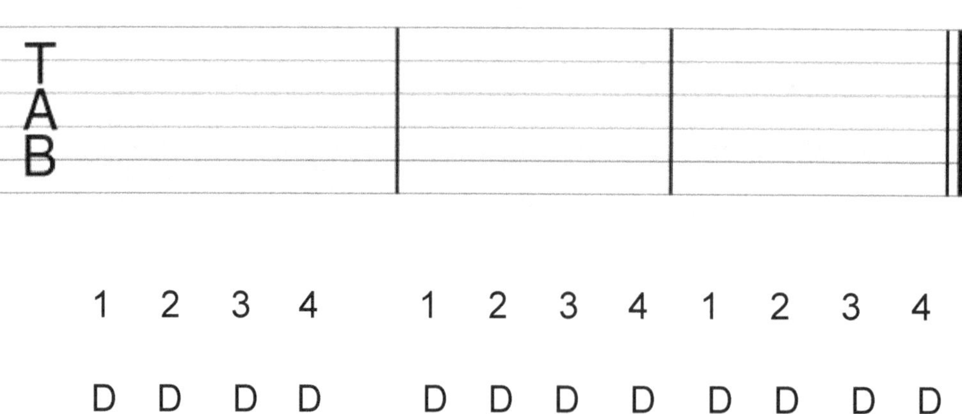

- **Down-Up-Down-Up:** Alternate between downstrokes and upstrokes for a smooth, flowing sound. This pattern is versatile and can be used in various musical styles.

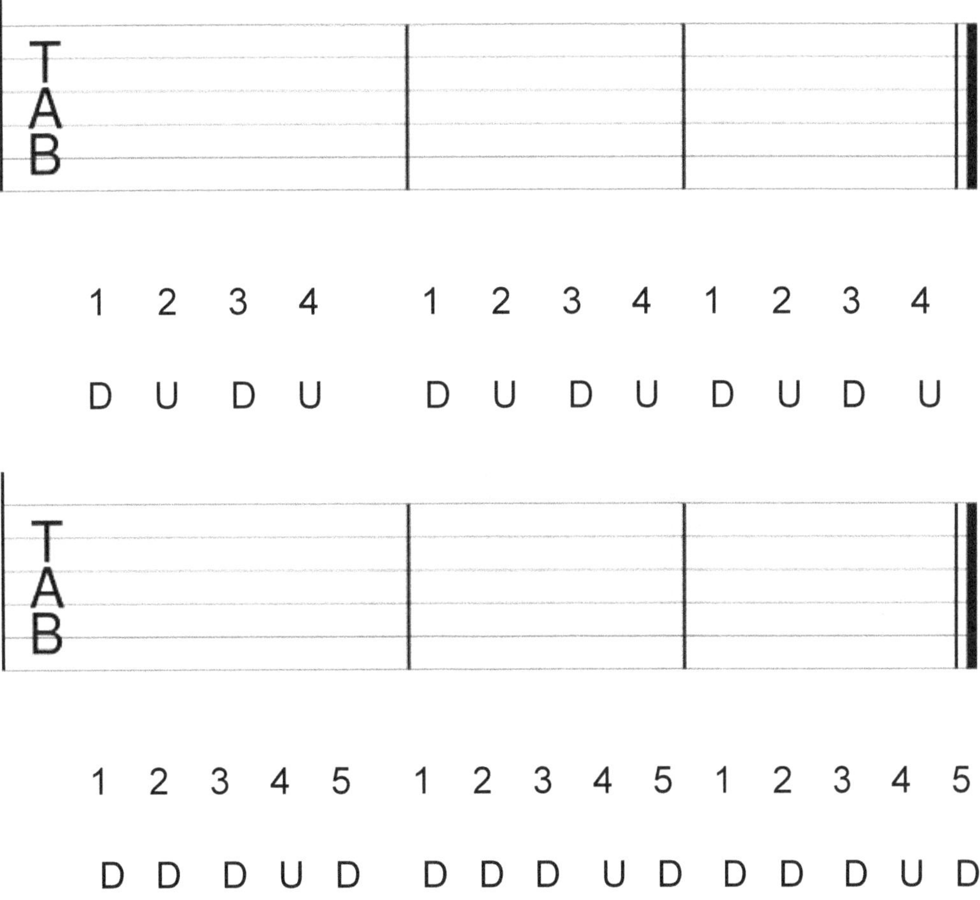

This last example uses both downstrokes and upstrokes to change up the rhythm. Learn these examples, and see if you can create ones of your own. For best results, practice daily.

Using a Pick

Using a pick, also known as a plectrum, is an essential skill for any guitarist. It allows for greater control, speed, and precision, making it ideal for both strumming and picking individual notes.

Holding the Pick

Properly holding the pick is crucial for achieving the best sound and maximizing control over your playing. Here's how to hold a pick correctly:

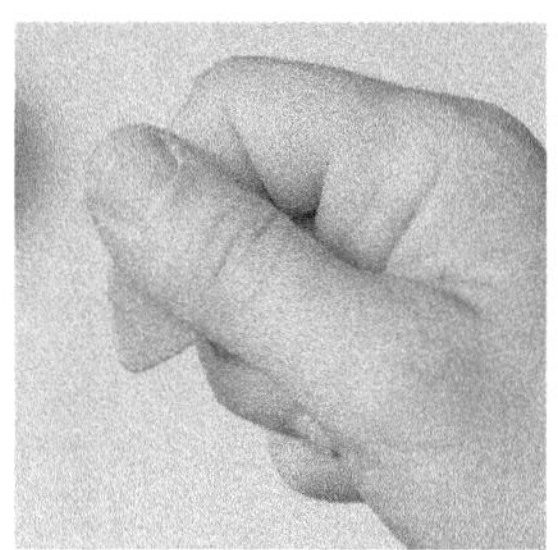 

Picks come in all different sizes, textures, and shapes. It is recommended that you try out a few. Finding the right one will make a huge difference.

By mastering the use of a pick, you'll enhance your ability to play both rhythm and lead guitar, making your music more dynamic and engaging.

Lesson 8: Rhythm and Timing

Mastering rhythm and timing is crucial for any guitarist, as they form your internal clock. Whether you're strumming chords, picking out melodies, or playing alongside other musicians, a strong sense of rhythm will ensure your playing is both accurate and expressive.

Understanding Rhythm

Rhythm refers to the pattern of sounds and silences in music. It's what makes music move and flow, providing structure and order. A strong sense of rhythm allows you to keep time, stay in sync with other musicians, and convey the intended feel of a piece.

Key Concepts

- **Beat:** The steady pulse of the music, much like a heartbeat. It's the fundamental time unit in a piece of music.
- **Tempo:** The speed at which a piece of music is played, usually measured in beats per minute (BPM).

- **Meter:** The grouping of beats into regular patterns, typically indicated by time signatures such as 4/4 or 3/4.

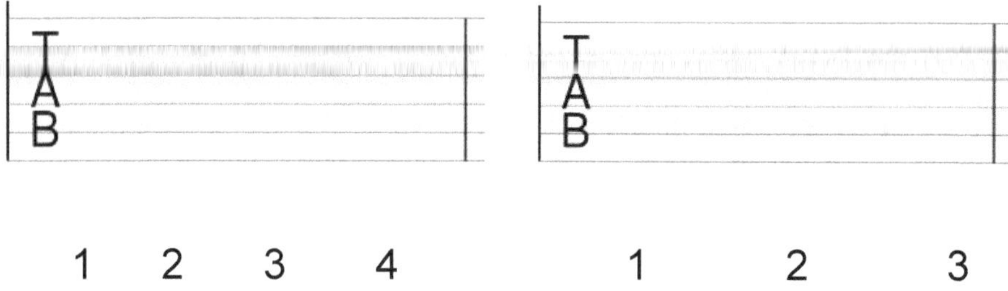

Keeping Time

Developing a strong internal sense of timing is essential for playing music accurately. Here are some strategies to help you keep time:

- **Count Aloud:** Counting the beats aloud while playing can help reinforce your timing and keep you on track.

 If you don't feel comfortable counting aloud, then count in your head.

- **Tap Your Foot:** Tapping your foot to the beat can provide a physical connection to the rhythm, helping you maintain a steady tempo.
- **Tap Your Foot:** Tapping your foot to the beat can provide a physical connection to the rhythm, helping you maintain a steady tempo.

Using a Metronome

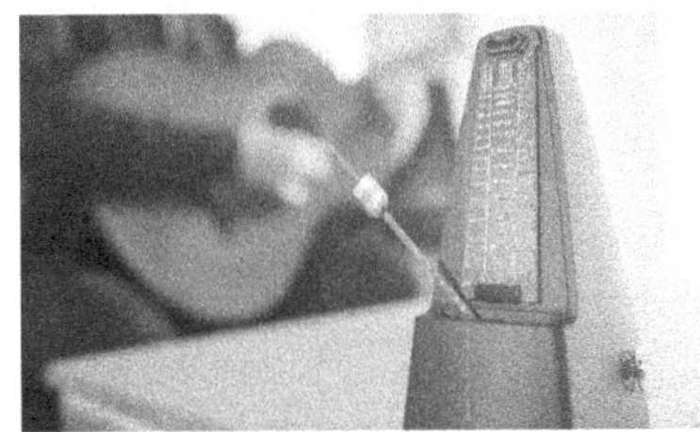

A metronome is an invaluable tool for any musician, providing a consistent beat for practice. Here's how to use it effectively:

- **Start Slow:** Begin at a slower tempo to ensure accuracy and gradually increase the speed as you become more comfortable.

Most people want to jump ahead, which causes problems later. Take it easy in the beginning to avoid this.

- **Practice Regularly:** Incorporate metronome work into your daily practice routine to build rhythmic precision.

Many people skip this concept as well and never build solid timing.

- **Experiment with Time Signatures:** Practice different time signatures to become comfortable with a range of rhythmic patterns.

Start with 4/4; this is what's called common time. Many, many songs are written in this time signature. Then proceed to the other ones.

- **Listen to Music:** Regularly listening to music can help you internalize different rhythms and tempos, enhancing your musical ear.

By focusing on rhythm and timing, you'll develop a solid foundation for your guitar playing, allowing you to play more confidently and expressively. As you continue to practice, you'll find yourself naturally locking into the groove, making your music more engaging and enjoyable. Keep practicing, and enjoy the rhythm of your musical journey!

Lesson 9: Chord Progressions

Chord progressions are the backbone of many songs, and understanding them is crucial for any guitarist. By learning common chord progressions, you'll be able to play a wide variety of songs and even start creating your own music.

Common Chord Progressions

One of the most popular chord progressions is the I-IV-V progression, often found in rock, pop, and blues music. In the key of G major, for instance, this would involve the chords G (I), C (IV), and D (V).

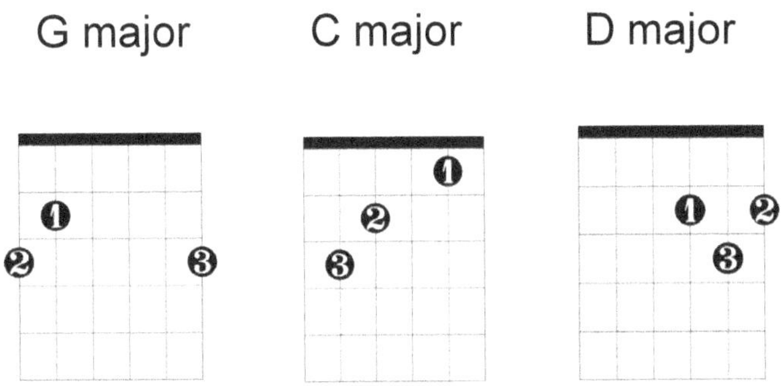

The 1-4-5 chord progression is the most common in Western music. Rock, Jazz, Folk, Country, and so forth. Work on this in different keys to get your ear familiar with it.

Another widely used progression is the ii-V-I, which is particularly prevalent in jazz music. In the key of C major, this would consist of the chords Dm (ii), G (V), and C (I). Practicing this progression in various keys will help you transition smoothly between chords.

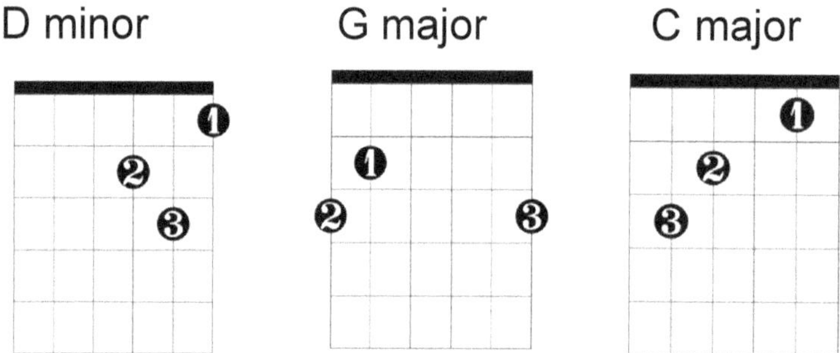

Like the other chord progression, work on this in different keys and with different chords to get familiar with how it sounds. This will not only help train your fingers to form chords, but also train your ear.

Remember, many, many songs are made up of only three chords. Think about this when you decide to compose your own song. These two progressions can be a great place to start.

Creating Your Own Progressions

Once you're comfortable with standard progressions, try experimenting to create your own. Start by picking a key and choosing a series of chords that sound pleasing to you. Remember, music is subjective, so trust your ear and don't be afraid to explore unusual combinations.

By mastering chord progressions, you'll gain a deeper understanding of how songs are structured and develop the ability to play and compose music more creatively.

Understanding the 12-Bar Blues

The 12-bar blues is a fundamental chord progression that underpins countless blues, rock, and jazz songs. This progression is named for its twelve-measure structure and is typically played in 4/4 time.

Mastering the 12-bar blues will not only enhance your understanding of musical form but also allow you to jam with other musicians and improvise with confidence.

42

The classic 12-bar blues progression uses three primary chords: the I, IV, and V chords of any given key. In the key of G major, these chords would be G (I), C (IV), and D (V). The progression is structured as follows:

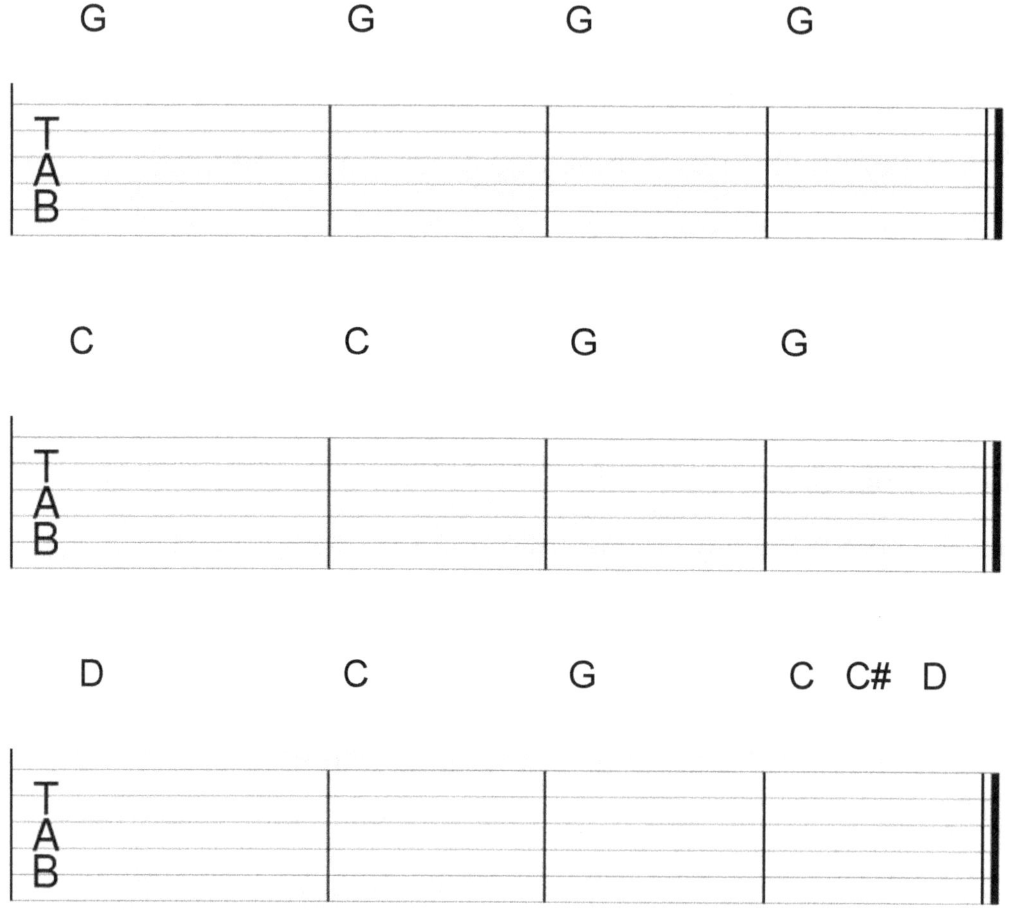

The last measure brings you back to the front to start over.

Chapter III Quiz

In Chapter 3, you have learned about basic strumming patterns, rhythm, timing, and chord progressions. All are designed to establish a solid foundation for quality rhythm playing.

Q: Why is the purpose of using downstrokes when strumming?

A: ____

Q: What is the purpose of using upstrokes when strumming?

A: ____

Q: What is the primary function of a metronome in practice?

A: ____

Q: In producing rhythm, what does the term tempo refer to?

A: ____

Q: In the key of C major, what chords make up the I, IV, and V?

A: ____

Q: What is the significance of the 12-bar blues progression?

A: ____

44

Chapter III summary

<u>First</u>, you learn about basic strumming patterns. Strumming is an essential technique for any guitarist, as it forms the rhythmic backbone of many songs. By mastering strumming patterns, you'll be able to add depth and texture to your playing.

<u>Second</u>, you learn about rhythm and timing. Mastering timing and rhythm is crucial for any guitarist, as they form your internal clock. A strong sense of rhythm will make sure your playing is accurate and expressive.

<u>Third</u>, you learn about chord progressions. This is where you put the chords together in a sequence to create harmony. By learning common chord progressions, you'll be able to play a wide variety of songs as well as compose your own.

<u>Fourth</u>, you learn about the importance of the 12-bar blues progression, and how hundreds of songs are made of this common sequence of three simple chords. A highly recommended place to start with progressions.

<u>Lastly</u>, by mastering chord progressions and creating your own, you'll build a better understanding of song composition. Remember, chords are the foundation, so the more you know about how to use them, the better guitarist you'll become.

Chapter IV: Introduction to Fingerpicking

Lesson 10: Fingerpicking Basics

Fingerpicking is a versatile and expressive technique that allows guitarists to create intricate and melodic sounds. Unlike strumming, which uses a pick to strike multiple strings simultaneously, fingerpicking involves plucking individual strings with your fingers.

By mastering this technique, you can add depth and complexity to your playing, making your music more engaging and dynamic.

Finger Placement

Proper finger placement is essential for effective fingerpicking. There are many different ways that guitarists do this, but here's a guide to help you position your fingers in the most common way. The classical way.

In this way, you will use your thumb, index, middle, and ring fingers. In this traditional fashion, the pinky is not used.

- **Thumb (P):** Use your thumb to pluck the bass strings (E, A, and D). The thumb provides a steady rhythm and is often responsible for the bass line in fingerpicking patterns.
- **Index Finger (I):** Place your index finger on the G string. It is typically used to pluck the middle strings, helping to create harmony.
- **Middle Finger (M):** Position your middle finger on the B string. This finger often plays the melody or supporting notes.
- **Ring Finger (A):** Use your ring finger for the high E
- string. It adds additional melodic or harmonic notes.

These two pictures show examples of fingerstyle. Notice the absence of the pick and the positioning of the fingers. Practice daily to get your fingers trained for proper positioning.

Basic Finger Patterns

Learning some basic fingerpicking patterns will help you get started and build confidence. Here are a few to practice:

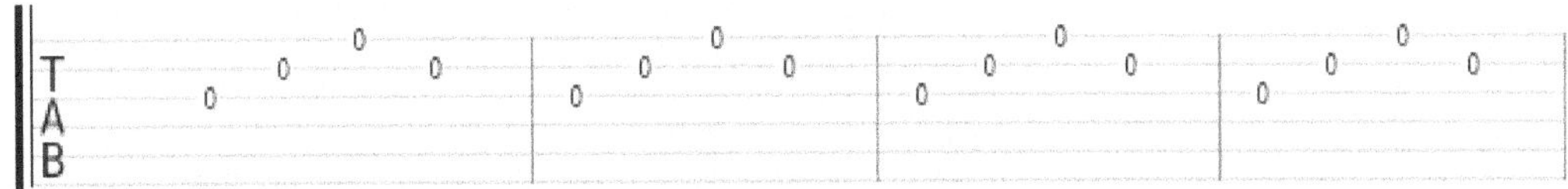

In this first example. You work on training the index, middle, and ring fingers to play the appropriate strings.

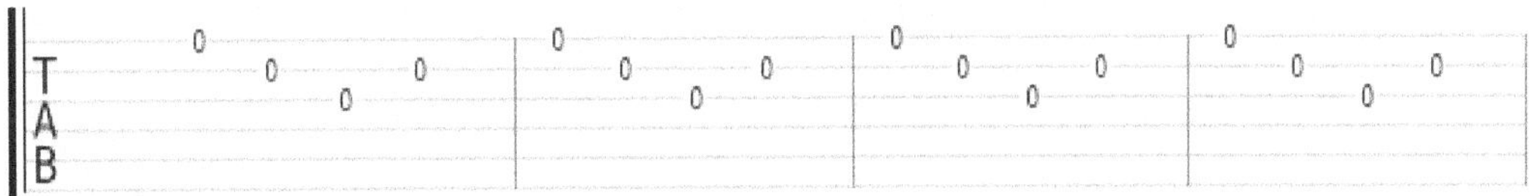

In this second example, you do the same thing, but you play them in a different order.

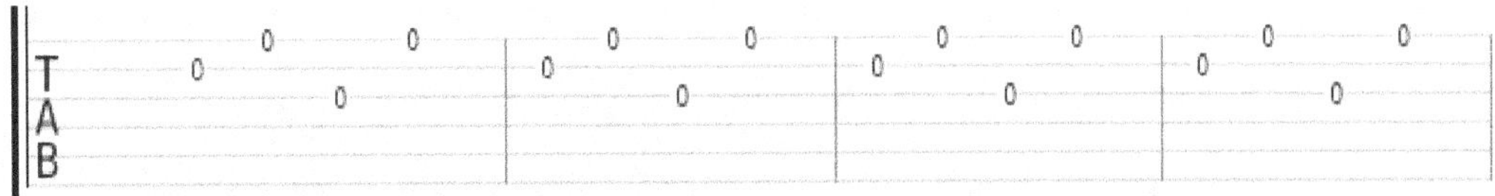

In this third example, you skip the second string and change up the pattern. This adds variety to the rhythm.

All three of these basic patterns should be practiced daily to train your fingers, develop timing, and build rhythm.

Tips for Practicing Fingerpicking

- **Start Slow:** Begin practicing these patterns slowly; this cannot be emphasised enough to ensure accuracy and precision. It will take time for your fingers to know which string to play.

Gradually increase your speed as you become more comfortable.

- **Use a Metronome:** Practice with a metronome to maintain a steady rhythm and improve your timing.

This is an excellent training tool for many applications, including fingerstyle. It is recommended that you get one and use it.

- **Focus on Clarity:** Ensure each note is clear and distinct. Avoid letting your fingers brush against adjacent strings to prevent unwanted noise. Relax and watch for tension.

By mastering these fingerpicking basics, you'll train your fingers to open a new realm of musical possibilities. As you continue, practice your technique, explore patterns and styles, and enrich your playing while expanding your musical repertoire.

Lesson 11: Developing Dexterity

Developing dexterity is crucial for any guitarist, as it enhances your ability to maneuver the fretboard with ease and precision. Improving dexterity will not only make you a more versatile player but also allow you to tackle more complex pieces as you advance in your musical journey.

Exercises for Flexibility

Flexibility is key to executing smooth transitions between chords and notes. Here are some exercises to help improve the flexibility of your fingers:

Spider Walk: Place your fingers on four consecutive frets on a single string. Lift each finger one at a time in a walking motion, moving up and down the string. This exercise promotes finger independence and flexibility.

```
      5   6   7   8
T                         5   6   7   8
A                                           5   6   7   8
B
```

Practice these five exercises daily to build dexterity, strength, and independence in your fingers.

- **Finger Stretching:** Gently stretch your fingers by placing them on the fretboard in wide intervals.

Practice stretching between the index and middle fingers, the middle and ring fingers, and the ring and pinky fingers to increase reach.

- **Scale Practice:** Play scales slowly and deliberately. Focus on maintaining a relaxed hand posture and using all four fingers.

Repeating scales helps improve finger agility and coordination.

Strengthening Fingers

Building finger strength is essential for maintaining consistent pressure on the strings and for producing clear, clean notes. Here are some ways to strengthen your fingers:

- **Finger Push-ups:** Place your fingertips on a table and press down as if doing a push-up.

This exercise can help build strength and endurance in your fingers.

- **Holding Chords:** Hold familiar chords for extended periods to ensure each note rings out clearly.

Instead of holding them for four counts, you hold them for eight. Gradually increase the duration to build stamina.

- **Grip Trainers:** Consider using a grip trainer or hand exerciser to strengthen the muscles in your fingers, hands, and forearms.

These tools, and many more like them, provide resistance training, helping you to build strength over time.

Tips for Developing Dexterity

- **Consistent Practice:** Dedicate daily time to practicing these exercises. Consistency is key to gradual improvement.

At first, it might seem hard, but over time, the fingers will limber up, the strength will build, and things will begin to happen.

- **Focus on Technique:** Pay attention to proper hand positioning and finger placement to avoid unnecessary tension.

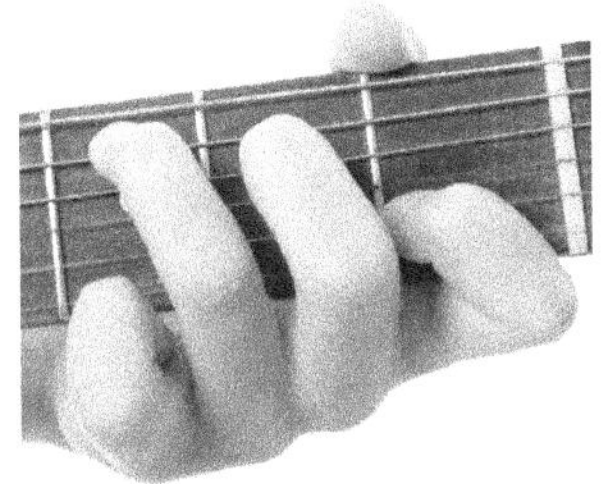

As you can see from the picture above, the fingers are curled in the front holding the C major chord, and the thumb is placed on top.

Here we have the D chord. Once again, the fingers are curled around the front, and the thumb is up on top. Giving you the best option for holding the strings down on the fretboard.

Remember, when playing open chords, you will need to use your fingertips.

- **Rest and Recovery:** Allow your hands to rest if you feel any strain or discomfort. Overworking your fingers can lead to injury.

It is always a good idea to take breaks. This gives your body and mind time to digest the new material and activities presented. Just make sure they are not too long, as this will hinder your progress.

- **Patience and Persistence:** Developing dexterity takes time, so be patient with your progress and persistent in your practice.

This cannot be stressed enough. As you progress in your studies, you'll discover that some things come easily, and others hard. So be patient and consistent in your practice.

By incorporating these exercises and tips into your practice routine, you'll enhance your dexterity, allowing for greater fluidity and expressiveness in your guitar playing. As you continue to build strength and flexibility, you'll find it easier to tackle more challenging pieces and expand your musical repertoire.

Lesson 12: Fingerpicking Styles

Fingerpicking is an art form that can transform your playing by adding depth and intricacy to your music. Exploring different fingerpicking styles will allow you to express yourself in various musical genres and enhance your versatility as a guitarist.

Thumb and Fingers

The fingerpicking style is characterized by its simplicity and rhythmic patterns. It's commonly used in folk, country, blues, and classical music and can accompany singing or storytelling. Here's how you can start practicing this style:

- **Alternating Bass and Treble:** Use your thumb to play the bass notes on the lower strings, while your index, middle, and ring fingers pluck the higher strings.

The use of the thumb creates a steady, alternating bass line that supports the melody and gives the impression of two instruments playing simultaneously. A very cool effect.

- **Travis Picking:** Named after Merle Travis, this technique involves a steady bass pattern with the thumb and syncopated treble notes with the fingers.

A common pattern is P-I-M-I, where the thumb plays a bass note, followed by the index and middle fingers playing the treble notes.

This example shows the thumb playing the bass strings while changing strings with each measure. The index and middle fingers will be playing the other two strings.

Remember, the thumb covers the bottom three strings. In the examples provided, the thumb will alternate between the three bass strings to build muscle memory and dexterity.

- **Roll Patterns:** Experiment with rolling patterns where the fingers pluck the strings in quick succession, creating a flowing arpeggiated effect. For example, try a P-I-M-A pattern with a smooth, continuous motion.

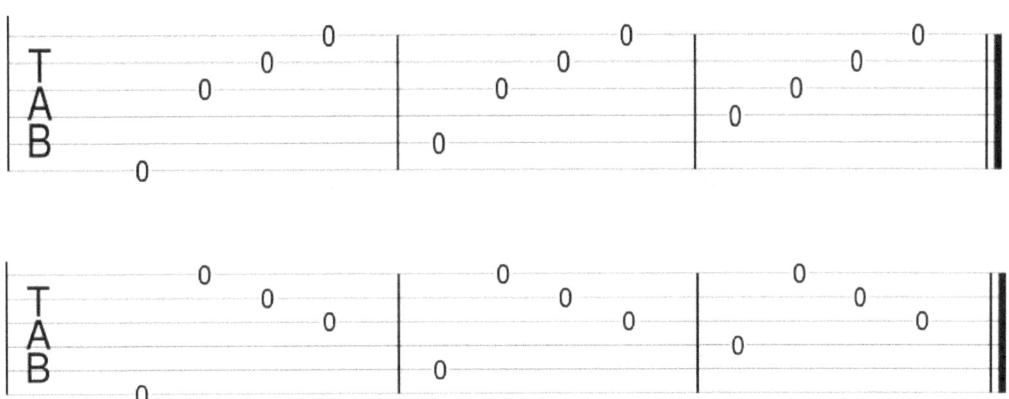

In these examples, you do the same thing as before, except you bring the use of the ring finger on the high E string. In example two, you go backwards.

Remember, this style of playing requires discipline. Especially classical music. So play these exercises multiple times to build strength, finger dexterity, and muscle memory.

Tips for Exploring Fingerpicking Styles

- **Listen to Influential Artists:** Explore recordings by renowned folk and classical guitarists to understand the nuances and expressiveness of each style

This will help train your ear to what it should sound like in songs and allow you to put that style into your own compositions.

- **Mix and Match:** Don't be afraid to blend elements from both styles to create your unique sound.

Experiment with different rhythms and patterns to fully grasp the technique and discover what works for you.

By exploring the style of fingerpicking, you'll enhance your ability to express emotions and tell stories through music, no matter if you're drawn to the simplicity of folk or the intricacy of classical.

Mastering these styles will significantly enrich your guitar playing experience. Keep practicing, and enjoy the journey of discovering new sounds and techniques!

Chapter IV Quiz

In Chapter 4, you have learned about fingerpicking basics, developing dexterity, and fingerpicking styles. All designed to enhance your playing and add diversity.

Q: What role does the thumb play in the style of fingerpicking?
A: ____

Q: What fingers are used in the P-I-M-A fingerpicking pattern?
A: ____

Q: What is the benefit of doing finger exercises daily?
A: ____

Q: What is a common exercise for building finger strength?
A: ____

Q: How does fingerpicking differ from using a pick?
A: ____

Q: What benefits are derived from mastering fingerpicking?
A: ____

Chapter IV Summary

First, you learn about fingerpicking basics. Fingerpicking is a versatile and expressive technique that lets you create intricate, melodic sounds. Using your fingers instead of a pick creates a softer, more subtle sound.

Second, you learn about developing finger dexterity. This is highly important for the fingerpicking technique, as each finger works independently of the others. Allowing you to tackle more complex musical pieces.

Third, you learn about different types of fingerpicking styles. By learning multiple ways to fingerpick, you'll be able to express yourself in various musical styles. As well as develop your picking hand for maximum proficiency.

Fourth, you learn to utilize your thumb and fingers together, with the thumb playing the bass notes and the fingers playing the treble notes. Listen to musical artists who incorporate this style into their playing to understand it better.

Lastly, practice patience, persistence, and discipline with this style of playing. It will help you develop your picking hand, expand your range of motion, and improve your overall musicianship.

Chapter V: Exploring Arpeggios

Lesson 13: What are Arpeggios?

Arpeggios are an essential technique for any guitarist, offering a way to play chords one note at a time and create a flowing, melodic sound.

Understanding and practicing arpeggios can greatly enhance your playing, adding texture and complexity to your music. Let's delve into the definition, use, and basic patterns of arpeggios.

Definition and Use

An arpeggio, often referred to as a "broken chord," involves playing the individual notes of a chord in succession rather than simultaneously.

This technique can be applied to any chord, allowing you to explore its tonal qualities more intimately. Arpeggios are used in a variety of musical genres, from classical to rock, and serve several purposes:

- **Melodic Lines:** Arpeggios can create melodic lines that weave in and out of a piece's harmonic structure, adding interest and complexity.

Transferring static chords into beautiful, flowing, vocal-like musical phrases.

- **Soloing:** In lead guitar playing, arpeggios are a valuable tool for creating solos that emphasize the chord changes within a song.

As a chord changes, you can focus on moving through the notes of the chords individually.

- **Accompaniment:** Arpeggios can provide a gentle, rhythmic accompaniment that supports the main melody or vocal line.

This is done by playing the notes of the chords individually instead of together, as in strumming. Giving you a much softer, ethereal type of guitar sound.

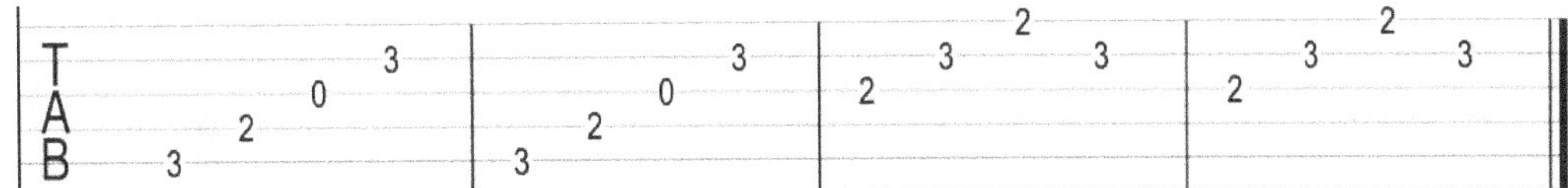

This first arpeggio example utilizes the C and D major chords.
The C is in the first two measures, and the D is in the last two.

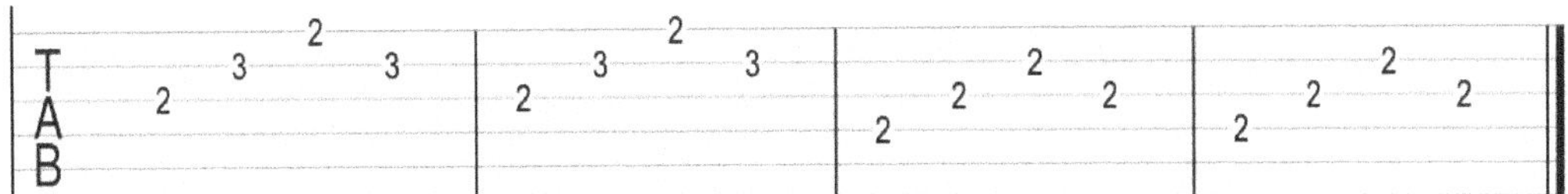

This second arpeggio example utilizes the D and A major
chords. This is also done with two measures each.

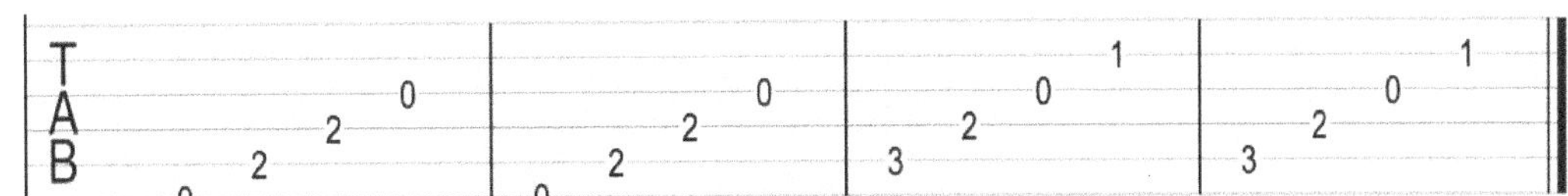

This third arpeggio example utilizes the E minor and C major
chords. This one allows you to play the sixth string open.

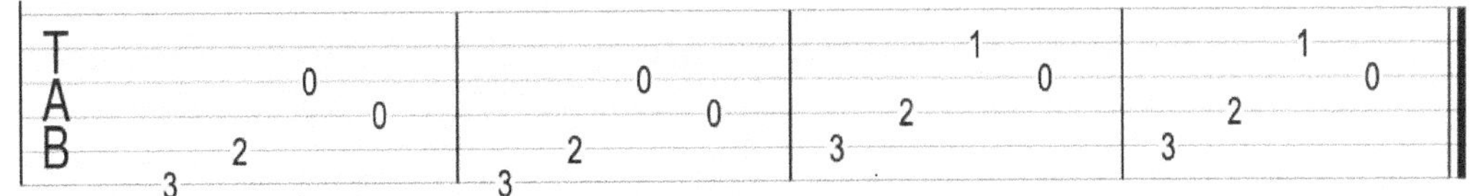

This last arpeggio example utilizes the G and C major chords.
This one lets you practice skipping a string.

Play these arpeggios daily, and work on crafting your own.

Tips for Practicing Arpeggios

- **Start Slowly:** Begin practicing arpeggios at a slow tempo to ensure accuracy and precision. Focus on clean, even notes.

Visualize the chord's shape for easier reference when playing the notes individually.

- **Use a Metronome:** Incorporate a metronome into your practice to maintain a consistent tempo and gradually increase your speed.

Metronomes are a great way not only to increase your speed but also to develop your timing and rhythm.

- **Focus on Clarity:** Ensure each note rings out clearly without overlapping or muting adjacent strings.

Make sure you practice forming chords with your fingertips so the open strings ring out.

By understanding and practicing arpeggios, you'll add a valuable technique to your musical toolkit, allowing you to explore new sounds and enhance your guitar playing.

Lesson 14: Practicing Arpeggios

Practicing arpeggios is a fundamental way to enhance your guitar skills, offering a pathway to more expressive and technically proficient playing. This lesson focuses on methods to improve your arpeggio technique, ensuring you can integrate this essential skill into your musical repertoire.

Slow Practice Techniques

Mastering arpeggios requires precision and control, which can be achieved through slow practice. Here are some techniques to guide you:

- **Focus on Technique:** Begin by playing each note slowly and deliberately. Concentrate on maintaining a consistent hand position and ensuring that each note is clear and distinct.

As a very important part of playing arpeggios, you must learn to develop patience and discipline.

- **Isolate Difficult Sections:** Identify any parts of the arpeggio pattern that are challenging. Isolate these sections and practice them repeatedly until they become smooth.

Make it a habit to break arpeggios down into smaller increments, then link them together as you get better with the technique.

- **Visualize Finger Movement:** Before playing, visualize the finger movements required for the arpeggio. This mental rehearsal can improve muscle memory and coordination.

Many aspects of playing guitar can be traced to visualization—chords, scales, and so forth. Learning to visualize their shape across the fretboard will help you to excel at playing them correctly.

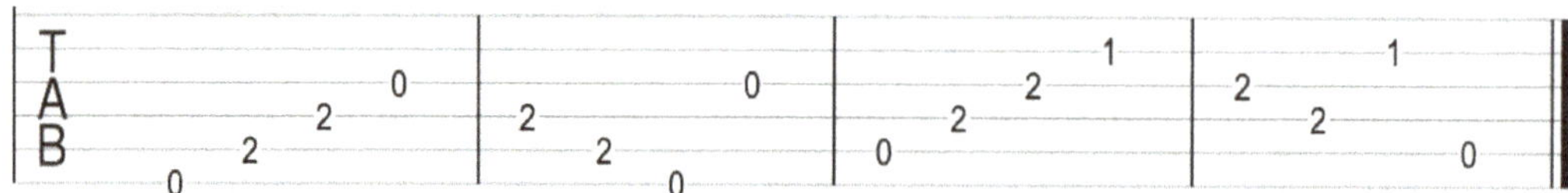

Here is another arpeggio example utilizing the E and A minor.

Increasing Speed

Once you've achieved accuracy and control at a slow tempo, gradually increasing speed can help you develop agility and confidence:

- **Incremental Tempo Increases:** Increase the metronome speed in small increments to ensure precision at each new tempo.

Avoid rushing the process; remember, patience is key. You must give it time to develop. That's why you move in small incremental steps.

- **Alternate Picking and Fingerpicking:** Practice both techniques to develop versatility. Alternate picking can help with speed, while fingerpicking offers a softer touch.

Utilizing both techniques also enhances your picking-hand skill and your overall musicianship.

Remember, the goal is to expand your playing ability, improve your technical skills, and enhance your approach to guitar playing.

Additional Arpeggio Tips

- **Consistent Practice:** Dedicate regular practice time to arpeggios and incorporate them into your daily routine.

Consistency will lead to steady improvement and a better understanding of the guitar fretboard.

- **Challenge Yourself:** Once comfortable with basic patterns, try tackling more complex arpeggios or increasing the tempo further.

Pushing your limits will expand your capabilities, unlock hidden potential, and help you develop your skills.

- **Stay Relaxed:** Tension can hinder speed and accuracy. Keep your hands and arms relaxed to prevent fatigue and reduce the risk of injury.

This will facilitate better control, improved endurance, and smoother playing ability.

By focusing on these arpeggio practice tips, you'll enhance your overall musicianship. Making your music more expressive and dynamic.

Lesson 15: Arpeggios and Strumming

Arpeggios and strumming are both essential techniques for any guitarist, offering distinct ways to create rhythm and texture in your music. By understanding and mastering these techniques, you'll enhance your ability to interpret songs and express yourself musically.

Integrating Arpeggios into Strumming Patterns

Combining arpeggios with strumming can add depth and interest to your playing. This technique allows you to highlight melodic lines in your strumming, creating a richer, more dynamic sound.

- **Identify Key Notes:** Begin by identifying the key notes within a chord that you want to emphasize. These notes will serve as the basis for your arpeggio pattern.

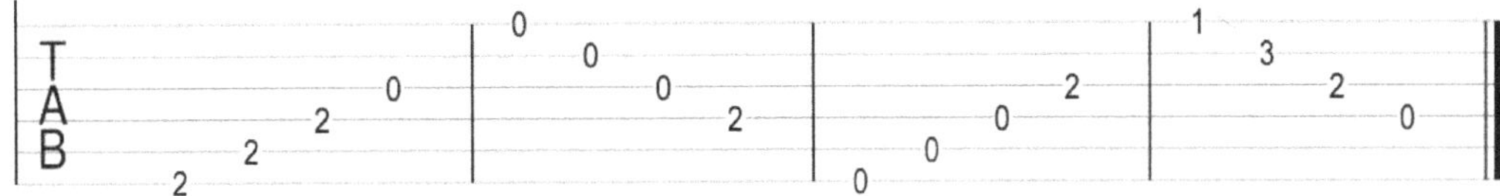

This arpeggio example emphasizes identifying key notes.

- **Use Simple Patterns:** Start with a simple arpeggio pattern, such as picking the bass note, then strumming a chord twice.

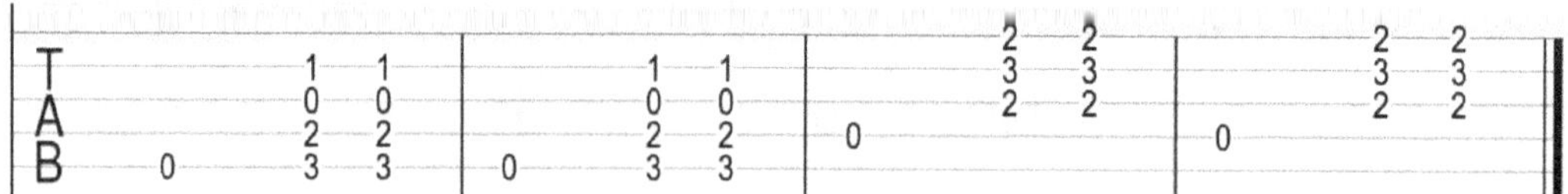

Here is an arpeggios strum example where you pick the bass note and strum a chord twice. This creates a syncopated rhythm with an odd feel.

Start with the arpeggio examples presented that have two chords. Once you have that technique down, work on arpeggiating some chords and strumming others.

This will add variety to your playing style. Once you are comfortable with that approach, gradually introduce more complex patterns as you become more proficient.

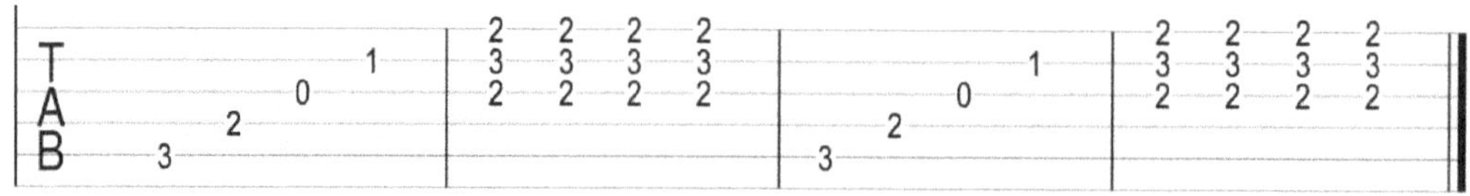

Here you arpeggiate the C major and strum the D major.

Transitioning Between Arpeggios and Strumming

Smoothly transitioning between arpeggios and strumming is a valuable skill that helps you maintain musical flow and adapt to different sections of a song. Here are some tips to help you transition seamlessly:

- **Practice Smooth Transitions:** Start slowly, focusing on the movement between picking and strumming.

Pay close attention to the transition between the two techniques. Gradually increase your speed as you gain confidence.

- **Focus on Hand Positioning:** Maintain proper hand positioning to ensure a smooth transition.

Your picking hand should be able to move easily between plucking individual strings and sweeping across all strings.

Transitioning between chords and individual techniques can be challenging at first. Give it time and be patient.

- **Use a Metronome**: Incorporate a metronome to maintain consistent timing during transitions. This can not be emphasized enough; that is why it keeps coming up.

It will allow you to progress by leaps and bounds if you put it into practice. Stay in rhythm and create a cohesive sound.

- **Incorporate into Songs**: Choose songs that naturally incorporate both arpeggios and strumming.

Practicing within a musical context will help solidify your ability to transition effectively. This approach will give you examples and ideas that you can use in your own songs.

Chapter V Quiz

In Chapter 5, you learned about exploring arpeggios. Arpeggio practice and combining arpeggios with strumming chords. This will enhance your guitar playing and mastery of the fretboard.

Q: What is the definition of an arpeggio?

A: ____

Q: What musical genres are arpeggios commonly used in?

A: ____

Q: What is a practice technique for mastering arpeggios?

A: ____

Q: How can visualizing finger movement help with practice?

A: ____

Q: What is the benefit of combining arpeggios with strumming?

A: ____

Q: How do you transition between arpeggios and strumming?

A: ____

74

Chapter V Summary

First, you learn about arpeggios. A creative way of playing guitar chords, different from strumming them. Arpeggios allow you to play chords one note at a time to create a flowing, melodic sound.

Second, you learn how to practice arpeggios. Mastering arpeggios requires precision and control. Which can be achieved through slow, daily practice of certain techniques, such as proper hand positioning and picking strings individually.

Third, you want to add arpeggios to your strumming technique. This gives you diversity in your playing while highlighting certain notes to create memorable melodic landscapes.

Fourth, arpeggios give you more control over your picking hand and force you to make sure you are forming your chords with proper finger positioning. If you ever want to know if you are forming your chords correctly, arpeggiate them.

Lastly, as with fingerpicking, make sure to give this technique time to develop. It will be a combination of both hands working together to create the desired sound, forming chords correctly, and picking the notes within them individually.

Chapter VI: Essential Guitar Maintenance

Lesson 16: String Maintenance

Proper string maintenance is essential for any guitarist, as it directly affects the sound and playability of your instrument. Taking care of your strings will ensure your guitar produces the best possible sound and prolongs the life of both the strings and the guitar.

Changing Strings

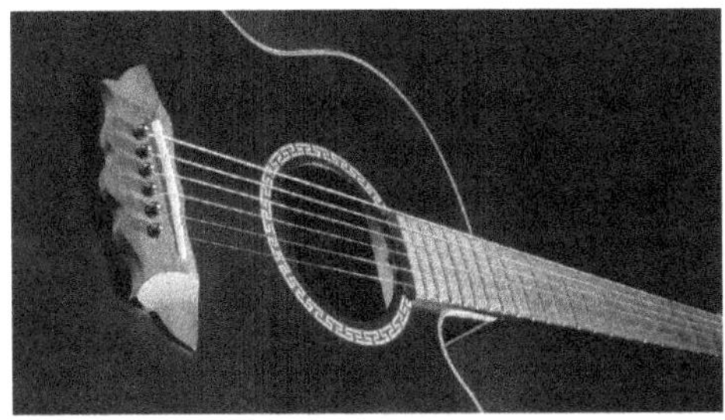

Regularly changing your guitar strings is crucial to maintaining a fresh, vibrant sound.

Old strings can become dull and difficult to play, affecting your overall performance. Here's a guide to help you change your strings effectively:

- **Gather Your Tools:** You'll need new strings, a string winder, wire cutters, and a tuner. Having these tools on hand will make the process smoother and more efficient.

- **Loosen and Remove Old Strings:** Use a string winder to loosen the tension of each string, then carefully unwind and remove them from the tuning pegs and bridge.

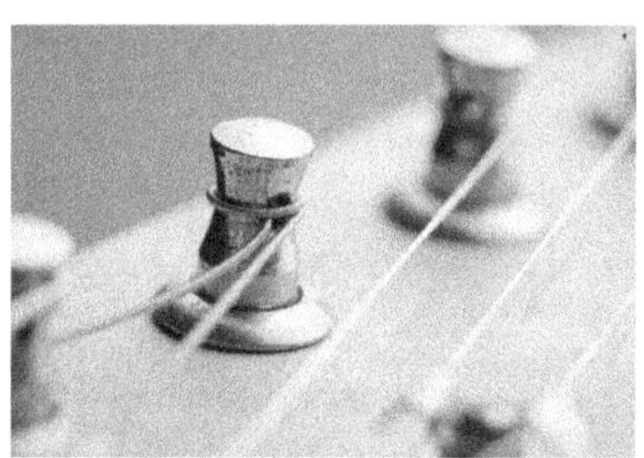

Be cautious of sharp ends as you remove the strings. These can poke your fingers and hinder your playing performance.

- **Tune the Strings:** Once all the strings are in place, use a tuner to bring each string up to pitch. Stretch each string gently by pulling it away from the fretboard to help it settle and maintain tuning stability.

Cleaning Strings

Regularly cleaning your strings can extend their lifespan and keep them sounding bright and lively. Here are some tips for keeping your strings clean:

- **Wipe Down After Playing:** Use a microfiber cloth to wipe down your strings after each playing session. This helps remove sweat, oils, and dirt that can lead to corrosion.

- **Use String Cleaner:** Apply a string cleaner or conditioner to further protect your strings and prevent buildup. Follow the manufacturer's instructions for best results.

Make sure to use the proper product, or the strings can be damaged. If you don't have string cleaner, just wipe them off with a dry cloth.

- **Wash Your Hands:** Before playing, wash your hands to minimize the amount of dirt and oils transferred to the strings.

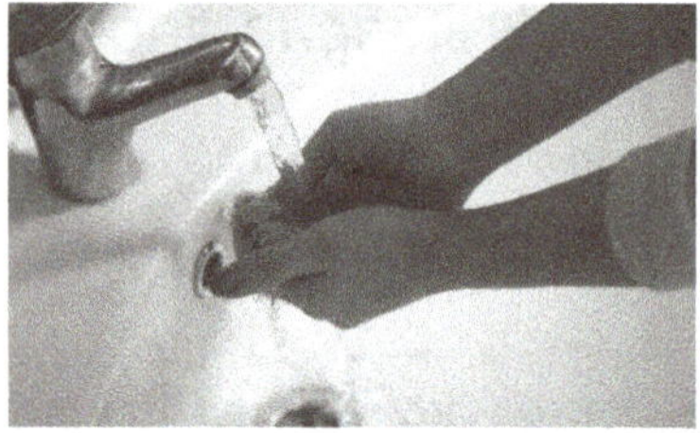

By practicing good string maintenance, you'll enhance the sound quality and playability of your guitar, making your musical experience more enjoyable. Regularly changing and cleaning your strings will ensure that your guitar continues to produce a bright, clear tone.

Lesson 17: Taking Care of the Body

Taking care of your acoustic guitar's body is essential for maintaining its appearance and sound quality over time. Proper maintenance will help protect your instrument from damage and ensure it continues to produce a rich, resonant sound.

Polishing the Body

Regularly polishing your guitar can keep it looking its best and help protect the finish. Here's how to do it effectively:

- **Choose the Right Polish:** Use a polish specifically designed for guitars. Avoid household cleaners, as they can damage the finish.

Quality guitar polish can remove scratches and oxidation.

- **Use a Soft Cloth:** Apply the polish with a clean, soft cloth, such as microfiber, to avoid scratching the surface. Always be careful when rubbing anything against the guitar body.

- **Polish Gently:** Rub the polish into the body in small, circular motions.

Pay special attention to areas that accumulate fingerprints and smudges.

- **Remove Excess Polish:** Use a separate clean cloth to gently buff the guitar, removing any excess polish and enhancing the shine.

Always have a cloth to apply the polish, and one to remove excess. This way, you can reuse them in the future for these specific purposes.

Proper Storage Techniques

Storing your guitar correctly is crucial to prevent damage and maintain its sound quality. Consider the following tips:

- **Use a Case or Gig Bag:** Always store your guitar in a hard case or padded gig bag when not in use. This protects it from dust, humidity, and accidental knocks.

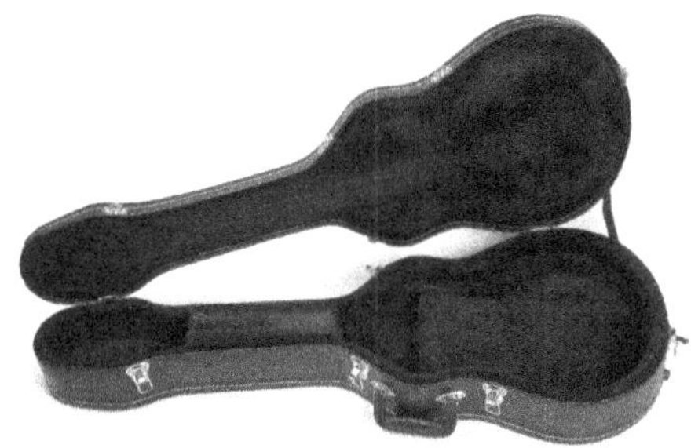

- **Control the Environment:** Keep your guitar in a room with stable temperature and humidity levels. Extreme changes can cause the wood to warp or crack. A humidifier or dehumidifier can help maintain optimal conditions.

By following these body care tips, you'll ensure your acoustic guitar remains in excellent condition, both visually and sonically.

Lesson 18: Neck and Fretboard Care

The neck and fretboard of your guitar are essential for playability and sound quality. Proper care and maintenance of these components will ensure that your guitar remains in optimal condition, allowing you to play comfortably and effectively.

Cleaning the Fretboard

Over time, dirt, oils, and grime can accumulate on the fretboard, affecting both its appearance and playability. Regular cleaning is essential to keep it in top condition. Here's how to clean your fretboard effectively:

- **Remove the Strings:** It's easiest to clean the fretboard when the strings are removed. This gives you full access to the entire surface.

- **Use a Soft Brush:** Gently brush away any loose dirt or dust. Be careful not to scratch the wood or damage the frets.

- **Apply Fretboard Cleaner:** Use a cleaner specifically designed for your fretboard's wood type. Apply it to a soft cloth and gently rub the fretboard.

Focus on areas around the frets where grime tends to build up. This comes from sweat and dirt on your fingers when playing the guitar over time.

- **Wipe and Buff:** Use a clean, dry cloth to wipe away any excess cleaner and buff the fretboard to a smooth finish. Do as you did with the body of the guitar. This step restores the wood's natural luster.

Additional Tips for Acoustic Guitar Care

- **Regular Maintenance:** Incorporate fretboard cleaning and minor adjustments into your regular guitar maintenance routine

This will help you to make it a habit to take care of your instrument.

- **Be Gentle:** Use gentle pressure when cleaning and adjusting to avoid causing damage.

Remember, the guitar is a finely crafted instrument, so handle it with care when playing and maintaining it.

- **Seek Professional Help:** If you feel unsure about maintaining your guitar, consider consulting a professional guitar technician. Incorrect maintenance can cause damage and prevent the guitar from performing as it should.

By taking care of the neck and fretboard, you'll enhance your guitar's playability and sound quality, ensuring it remains a reliable instrument for your musical journey.

Chapter VI Quiz

In Chapter 6, you have learned about string maintenance, care for the body, neck, and fretboard. Allowing you to ensure your guitar performs at its best at all times.

Q: Why is it important to change your strings regularly?
A: ____

Q: What material should you use to clean your guitar strings?
A: ____

Q: What type of polish should be used on your guitar body?
A: ____

Q: Why is the climate where you store your guitar important?
A: ____

Q: Why is it important to keep the guitar properly adjusted?
A: ____

Q: What should you use when applying fretboard cleaner?
A: ____

Chapter VI Summary

First, you learn about proper string maintenance. This is highly important to learn, as the vibration of the guitar strings is how the instrument produces its sound. Proper string care ensures the guitar produces a high quality tone.

Second, just like the strings, you also want to take care of the body. Taking care of the guitar body is essential for maintaining its appearance and sound quality over time. Polishing it regularly will help it look its best and protect the finish.

Third, you learn about the neck and fretboard. Keeping these clean and properly adjusted will ensure the best performance from the guitar. Over time, dirt, oil, and grime can accumulate on the fretboard, and it will need to be cleaned properly.

Fourth, use a high-quality string set for the best tonal output. Make sure to also use quality materials for cleaning and caring for the instrument. Keep them handy when needed, and use proper cleaners for the body and fretboard.

Lastly, the more you know about your instrument and how to care for it, the more you'll appreciate it. This way, it will perform at its best when the time is right. Remember, the guitar is an extension of you and how you choose to express yourself.

Chapter VII: Developing Practice Habits

Lesson 19: Setting Practice Goals

Setting practice goals is a crucial step in your guitar learning journey. Well-defined goals provide direction and motivation, helping you track your progress and stay focused.

By setting both short-term and long-term goals, you can ensure steady improvement and maintain a sense of achievement as you progress.

Short-term Goals

Short-term goals are achievable objectives that you can work towards in a relatively short period, usually within weeks or a few months.

These goals help maintain momentum and provide quick wins that boost motivation. Here are some examples of short-term goals:

- **Master a New Chord:** Set a goal to learn and master a new chord each week. Focus on finger positioning and smooth transitions to incorporate it seamlessly into your playing.

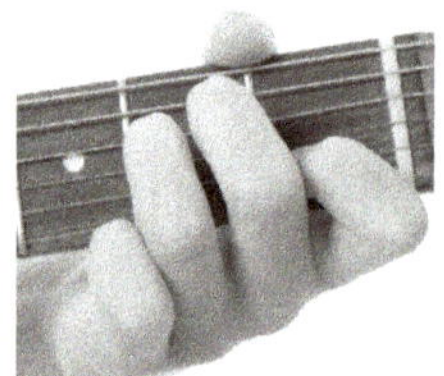

Proper finger placement goes a long way toward playing efficiently. Make sure to spend time on this. Will will pay dividends in the long run.

- **Develop Finger Strength:** Dedicate a few minutes each day to finger exercises designed to build strength and dexterity, such as scales or chord transitions.

```
      5   6   7   8
T                        5   6   7   8
A                                            5   6   7   8
B
```

It is highly recommended that you work on finger exercises daily to develop dexterity, strength, and muscle memory.

Long-term Goals

Long-term goals are broader objectives that take more time and effort to achieve, often spanning several months or even years. These goals provide a vision for your overall growth as a guitarist.

- **Build a Repertoire:** Aim to learn and memorize a set number of songs across different genres and styles.

Create a personal repertoire that you can perform well. This will help to build self-confidence.

- **Achieve Technical Mastery:** Set a goal to master advanced techniques such as barre chords, alternate tunings, or fingerstyle playing.

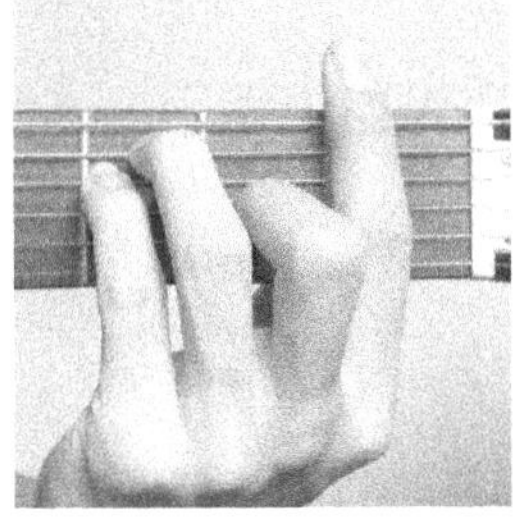 

Break these techniques into manageable steps and work on them consistently for quicker, better results.

Lesson 20. Effective Practice Routines

Developing effective practice routines is essential for maximizing your progress as a guitarist. A well-structured practice routine helps you focus on specific skills, build consistency, and ensure that your time spent practicing is productive and enjoyable.

Warm-up Exercises

Warming up is a crucial part of any practice session, as it prepares your fingers, hands, and mind for playing. Incorporate these exercises into your routine to ensure a productive session:

- **Finger Stretches:** Begin with gentle finger stretches to improve flexibility and prevent strain. This can include stretching your fingers apart and gently bending them back.

- **Scales:** Practice simple scales to warm up your fingers and improve your finger positioning and muscle memory. Start with basic major and minor scales, gradually introducing more complex variations.

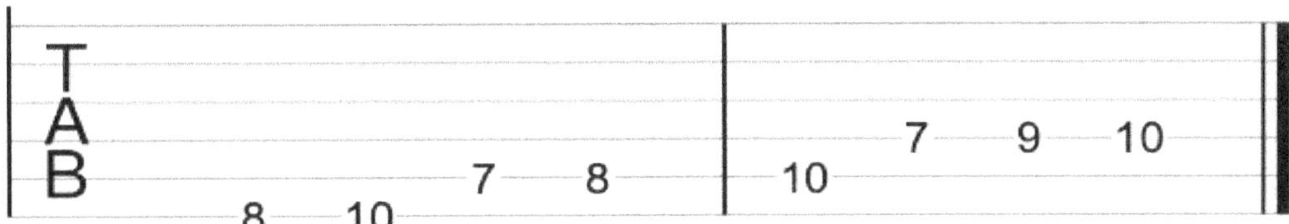

This is the C major scale played at the 8th fret. A great place to start playing scales and understanding music.

- **Arpeggios:** Incorporate arpeggio patterns to warm up both your picking hand and fretting hand, enhancing synchronization and accuracy.

These were gone over previously. Go back and work on them if needed. These are a great way to develop your picking hand and add diversity to your guitar playing.

Remember, to work on all four fingers on both hands if you can. This will give you the best option for unlocking the fretboard.

Structured Sessions

A structured practice session ensures that you cover all necessary areas of your guitar learning journey. Here's how you can organize your practice time effectively:

- **Set Clear Objectives:** Begin each session with specific goals in mind, such as mastering a new chord, improving a particular technique, or learning part of a song.

This focus will guide your practice, help you make the best use of your time, and prevent aimless playing.

- **Divide Your Time:** Allocate time to different aspects of your playing, such as technique, songs, improvisation, and theory.

For instance, spend 10 minutes on scales, 20 minutes on chord transitions, and 15 minutes on song practice.

By doing this, you accomplish more in multiple areas that need improvement, while avoiding playing the same easy things over and over, which is very common and not recommended. Work on what needs improving as well.

- **Focus on Weaknesses:** Identify areas for improvement and dedicate extra time to them. This targeted practice will help you overcome challenges more efficiently.

Focus on what needs improvement, as this will give you the best chance to improve your proficiency.

- **Mix It Up:** Include a variety of exercises and songs to keep your practice sessions engaging and prevent monotony. This variety will keep you engaged with different aspects of guitar playing and help you develop a more well-rounded skill set.

Remember, the key is to balance discipline with creativity, allowing you to explore new techniques while honing your skills.

By establishing an effective practice routine, you'll ensure steady progress, with less time wasted, and a more enjoyable learning experience on your acoustic guitar journey. Allowing you to become a more proficient player.

Lesson 21: Staying Motivated

Staying motivated is key to your success and enjoyment as a guitarist. The journey of learning an instrument is filled with both rewarding moments and challenges, and maintaining motivation will help you persevere through the ups and downs.

Let's explore strategies to sustain your enthusiasm and keep your practice engaging and fulfilling.

Setting Realistic Expectations

One of the most important aspects of staying motivated is setting realistic expectations for your progress. Recognize that learning an instrument is a gradual process, and it's normal to encounter plateaus or difficulties along the way.

- **Embrace the Process:** Understand that improvement takes time and effort. Celebrate small victories and acknowledge that every practice session contributes to your growth.

- **Avoid Comparisons:** Focus on your own journey rather than comparing yourself to others. This is what's great about self-study. You get to progress at your own speed. Everyone learns at their own pace, and your progress is unique to you. So make sure to embrace this as you study.

Finding Joy in Practice

Keeping your practice sessions enjoyable will help sustain your motivation. Incorporate elements that make playing the guitar fun and rewarding.

- **Experiment with Different Styles:** Explore different genres and styles to keep things fresh. Every style approaches the guitar differently.

Trying new techniques or musical styles can reignite your passion and curiosity. It also keeps you from getting bored playing the same things over and over again.

Usually, the things that you're already good at.

Overcoming Challenges

Facing challenges is a natural part of learning the guitar. Developing strategies to overcome obstacles will help you stay motivated and continue progressing.

- **Break Down Difficulties:** When faced with a challenging piece or technique, break it down into smaller, manageable parts.

Focus on mastering each section before putting it all together. Then focus on new challenges to keep yourself engaged.

- **Stay Positive:** Maintain a positive mindset and remind yourself of your progress.

Use setbacks as opportunities to learn and grow, rather than as reasons to give up.

By incorporating these strategies, you'll be able to maintain your motivation and enjoy the journey of learning the guitar. Remember, the key is to find joy in the process, celebrate your progress, and keep pushing forward. Practice daily, and you'll enjoy the music you create along the way!

Chapter VII Quiz

In Chapter 7, you learned about setting practice goals, effective practice routines, and staying motivated. All designed to make the best out of your time while continuing to move forward.

Q: What is the benefit of setting short-term practice goals?

A: ____

Q: What is the benefit of setting long-term practice goals?

A: ____

Q: Why is a warm-up exercise important in a practice session?

A: ____

Q: What strategy works for a productive practice session?

A: ____

Q: What is one way to keep your practice session enjoyable?

A: ____

Q: How can you overcome challenges on your guitar journey?

A: ____

Chapter VII Summary

<u>First</u>, you learn about the importance of setting practice goals. Well-defined goals provide direction and motivation. Helping you track your progress, stay focused, and make the best use of your time.

<u>Second</u>, you learn that developing a practice routine is essential. As this ensures you practice what is needed to get you where you want to go, without wasting time on things that will not get you there.

<u>Third</u>, you learn how to stay motivated. This is very important as there will be many hurdles and challenges along your journey. Knowing how to stay motivated and keep moving forward during these times will help you to conquer them.

<u>Fourth</u>, one way to stay motivated is for you to set realistic expectations for your progress. Recognize that learning the guitar is a gradual process, and any challenges you experience are normal.

<u>Lastly</u>, staying motivated is a lot easier said than done. Just focus on your own journey and don't compare yourself to others. A very common thing that kills motivation. Just keep putting one foot in front of the other, and you'll get there.

Chapter VIII: Bringing it All Together

Lesson 22: Basic Scale Theory

Understanding scale theory is fundamental for any guitarist, as scales form the backbone of melodies, harmonies, and improvisation. By grasping the basics of scales, you'll be able to expand your musical vocabulary and enhance your ability to create and play music.

Major and Minor Scales

Major Scales

The major scale is one of the most common and important scales in Western music. It provides a bright and cheerful sound and serves as the foundation for many songs and compositions. The major scale is constructed using a specific pattern of whole steps (W) and half steps (H):

- **Pattern: W-W-H-W-W-W-H**
- **For example, the C major scale follows this pattern and includes the notes: C, D, E, F, G, A, and B.**

Minor Ocales

The minor scale, on the other hand, offers a more somber and melancholic sound. There are three types of minor scales: natural, harmonic, and melodic. Each has its unique pattern:

- **Natural Minor Scale: W-H-W-W-H-W-W**
- **Harmonic Minor Scale: W-H-W-W-H-W½-H**
- **Melodic Minor Scale (Ascending): W-H-W-W-W-W-H**

For instance, the A natural minor scale consists of the notes: A, B, C, D, E, F, and G.

Scales are often presented in box patterns. Below is the major and minor scale box pattern.

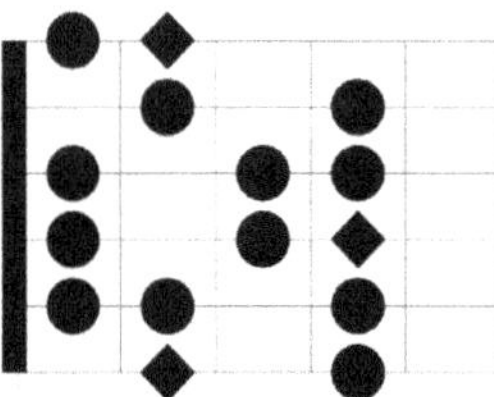 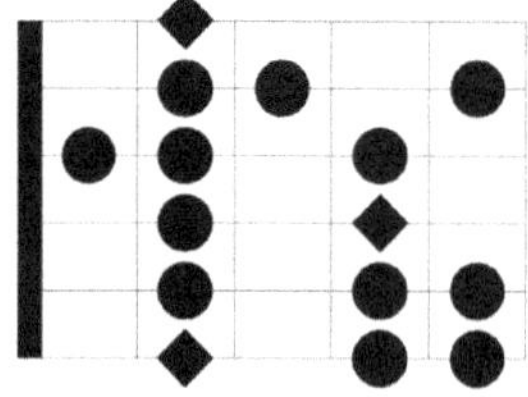

The Major Scale   The Minor Scale

Reading these is just like reading guitar tab; the biggest string is on the bottom. These can be played anywhere along the neck.

Pentatonic Scales

Major Pentatonic Scale

The major pentatonic scale is a five-note scale derived from the major scale. It is popular in many musical genres due to its simplicity and pleasing sound. The major pentatonic scale omits the fourth and seventh notes of the major scale:

C Major Scale: C D E F G A B = 1 2 3 4 5 6 7

C Major Pentatonic: C D E G A = 1 2 3 5 6

Minor Pentatonic Scale

The minor pentatonic scale is similar and is particularly common in blues and rock music. It is derived from the natural minor scale by omitting the second and sixth notes:

A Minor Scale: A B C D E F G = 1 2 b3 4 5 b6 b7

A Minor Pentatonic: A C D E G = 1 b3 4 5 b7

Notice how you use just five notes from the major and minor scales to make the pentatonic scales. This makes them easier to learn and provides a wider range of use.

Tips for Practicing Scales

- **Start Slowly:** Practice scales slowly to ensure accurate finger placement and clear note articulation.

Gradually increase your speed as you become more comfortable.

- **Use a Metronome:** Incorporate a metronome to maintain consistent timing and improve your rhythmic precision.

A metronome is an excellent learning tool that should be part of your learning arsenal.

- **Explore Different Positions:** Practice scales in various positions on the fretboard to gain familiarity with different fingerings and expand your playing range.

This will help you master the fretboard and expand your ear training. Also, scales can provide a solid foundation for improvisation, experimenting with creating melodies and solos over chord progressions.

The Major Scale: 1 2 3 4 5 6 7

The Natural Minor Scale: 1 2 b3 4 5 b6 b7

The Melodic Minor Scale: 1 2 b3 4 5 6 7

The Harmonic Minor Scale: 1 2 b3 4 5 b6 7

The Major Pentatonic Scale: 1 2 3 5 6

The Minor Pentatonic Scale: 1 b3 4 5 b7

Notice how the minor scales all have a flat third note. This is what gives them their sad, somber sound. The major scales have a natural third note, which gives them their happy upbeat tone, and the pentatonic scales are made up of only five notes.

Notice also that the melodic and harmonic minor scales are alternates of the natural minor. This gives each of them a different type of musical tone.

Now, you have two major scales and 4 minor scales to work with. These scales will provide you with a solid foundation for playing solos and melody lines, as they are the most common found in songs.

Lesson 23: Basic Chord Theory

Now that we know the basics of scale theory, let's take a look at the basics of chord theory. By grasping the basics of how chords are constructed and function within a musical context, you'll gain the tools to expand your playing repertoire and enhance your creativity.

Chord Construction

Chords are essentially a combination of notes played simultaneously, creating harmony. Knowing how these chords are constructed can help you both learn existing songs and compose your own music. Here are the basics of chord construction:

- **Triads:** Most common chords are triads, consisting of three notes. These notes are the root, the third, and the fifth.

For example, in a C major chord, the notes are C (root), E (third), and G (fifth). C major = 1 3 5.

- **Major and Minor Chords:** The difference between major and minor chords lies in the third. A major chord has a natural third, and a minor chord has a flat third.

The major triad = 1 3 5, and the minor triad = 1 b3 5.

- **Chord Extensions:** Beyond triads, chords can have additional notes, known as extensions, such as sixths, sevenths, and ninth chords.

These add richness and complexity to the harmony. For example, a C7 chord includes the notes C, E, G, and B flat.

The C7 chord: 1 3 5 b7 = C E G Bb. With a seven chord, you will flatten the seventh note within the key to give this chord its particular sound.

The sixth and ninth chords use the same concept; they use additional notes from the key to create them.

C major sixth: 1 3 5 6 = C E G A

C add-nine: 1 3 5 9 = C E G D

The D note in the second octave represents the ninth note.

Chord Functions

Understanding how chords function within a key is essential for creating progressions and understanding music theory. Here are the primary functions of chords:

- **Tonic (I):** The tonic chord is the home chord in a progression. It provides a sense of resolution and rest. In the key of C major, the tonic chord is C major.

The tonic chord, also called the root note, is the base of the chord and is not usually altered.

- **Dominant (V):** The dominant chord creates tension that typically resolves to the tonic. It's built on the fifth degree of the scale.

In C major, the dominant is G major. The reason for this is that the G note is the fifth in the key of C major.

Key of C major: C D E F G A B

- **Subdominant (IV):** The subdominant chord often precedes the dominant, providing a transition. It's built on the fourth degree of the scale. In C major, the subdominant is F major.

The subdominant chord moves away from the tonic to create tension, leading to the dominant chord.

- **Other Functions:** Chords also serve additional roles, such as the supertonic (ii), mediant (iii), and submediant (vi), each adding variety and movement to progressions.

A Tip for Applying Chord Theory

- **Practice Progressions:** Use common progressions like I-IV-V or ii-V-I to hear how different chords function together and create a musical narrative.

Remember, chord progressions are the foundation of songs. The more you know in this area, the better you'll be.

By mastering basic chord theory, you'll gain a deeper understanding of music, enhancing both your playing and compositional skills.

Lesson 24: Performing for Others

Performing for others is a significant milestone in any guitarist's journey. It offers an opportunity to share your music, connect with an audience, and gain valuable experience that can enhance your playing.

Overcoming Stage Fright

Stage fright is a common experience for many musicians, regardless of their level of expertise. Managing these nerves is crucial to performing confidently and enjoying the experience. Here are some strategies to help you overcome stage fright:

- **Preparation is Key:** Thoroughly prepare for your performance by practicing your set multiple times.

Knowing your material inside out will boost your confidence and reduce anxiety. Always be prepared.

- **Start Small:** Begin by performing in front of friends or family to build your confidence. Gradually increase your audience size as you become more comfortable performing.

- **Breathing Techniques:** Practice deep breathing exercises to calm your nerves before stepping on stage. Slow, deep breaths can help reduce stress and keep you focused.

Starting small and practicing breathing exercises will give you the best chance of preparing and reducing anxiety.

- **Accept Imperfection:** Remember that making mistakes is a natural part of performing. If you make an error, keep going and maintain your composure.

Audiences are often more forgiving than you might think. At first, don't put too much pressure on yourself. It will get better over time.

Engaging an Audience

Engaging your audience is essential to creating a memorable performance. By connecting with your listeners, you'll make your music more impactful and enjoyable.

- **Make Eye Contact:** Establish a connection with your audience by making eye contact.

This simple gesture can create a sense of intimacy and make listeners feel more involved in your performance.

- **Tell a Story:** Share brief anecdotes or insights about the songs you're performing. Providing context or a personal story can make your performance more relatable and engaging.

Storytelling is a big part of a song becoming a hit. If you want to sing as well as play, perfect your storytelling.

- **Body Language:** Use expressive body language to convey the emotions of your music. Move naturally with the rhythm and let your enthusiasm shine through.

- **Interact with the Audience:** Encourage audience participation by inviting them to clap or sing along to familiar parts of a song.

This interaction can foster a lively, collaborative atmosphere and make for a more memorable listening experience.

- **Be Authentic:** Be yourself on stage. Authenticity resonates with audiences, making your performance more genuine and memorable.

By focusing on these aspects of performing, you'll be able to overcome stage fright, engage your audience, and deliver a compelling performance. Remember, performing is an opportunity to share your passion and connect with others through music. Embrace the experience, and enjoy the journey of bringing your music to life on stage!

Lesson 25: Continuing Your Guitar Journey

As you reach the end of this guide, it's important to recognize that learning the guitar is a lifelong journey filled with endless opportunities for growth and exploration.

Whether you're a beginner who's just starting out or a more seasoned player looking to expand your skills, there are always new paths to pursue.

Exploring Advanced Techniques

Now that you have a solid foundation, you can delve into more advanced techniques to further enhance your playing:

- **Fingerstyle and Hybrid Picking:** Explore intricate fingerstyle techniques or hybrid picking, which combines a pick and fingers.

These methods can add complexity and texture to your playing, allowing for greater expression. Once you get down using a pick and fingerstyle individually, work at putting them together for a more advanced approach.

- **Alternate Tunings:** Experiment with alternate tunings like Drop D, Open G, or DADGAD to discover new sounds and expand your musical vocabulary.

Example of Open G Tuning: D G D G B D

Each tuning offers unique possibilities for chord voicings and melodic exploration because the notes change positioning along the fretboard. This allows the instrument to create a different sound and to expand creativity.

- **Advanced Chord Voicings:** Learn more complex chord shapes, such as suspended, augmented, and diminished chords, to add depth and sophistication to your music.

An augmented triad is where you sharpen the fifth note of the triad, and a diminished triad is where you flatten both the third and fifth notes. With suspended chords, you move the third.

Seeking Further Education

To continue growing as a guitarist, consider seeking additional educational resources and opportunities:

- **Private Lessons:** If possible, take private lessons with an experienced guitar teacher who can provide personalized guidance and feedback tailored to your goals.

- **Online Courses and Tutorials:** Explore online platforms that offer video lessons and tutorials. These resources can offer valuable insights and techniques from professional guitarists worldwide.

- **Music Theory:** Deepen your understanding of music theory to enhance your compositional skills and ability to communicate with other musicians. This knowledge will empower you to analyze and create more sophisticated music.

- **Workshops and Masterclasses:** Attend workshops and masterclasses to learn from accomplished musicians. These events provide opportunities to gain new perspectives and connect with other guitarists.

Embark on your journey with excitement and work on these aspects of your learning to make it more enjoyable.

Chapter VIII Quiz

In Chapter 8, you learned about basic scale theory, basic chord theory, and performing for others. These lessons will enhance your musicianship and help to build self-confidence.

Q: What is the whole step, half step pattern in the major scale?
A: ____

Q: What makes the minor scale different from the major?
A; ____

Q: What three notes from a musical key make up a triad?
A: ____

Q: In the key of C major, what is the function of the G chord?
A: ____

Q: How can you engage your audience during a performance?
A; ____

Q: How can you stay motivated and keep growing?
A: ____

Chapter VIII Summary

First, you learn about basic scale theory. Understanding scale theory is fundamental for any guitarist, as it provides the backbone for solos, melodies, and improvisation. Allowing you to expand your musical vocabulary.

Second, you learn about basic chord theory. Understanding chord theory is fundamental for any guitarist as well. It provides the backbone for chord construction, chord extensions, harmonies, and chord progressions.

Third, you learn the fun of playing for others. Remember, music is an art form that's meant to be shared and passed on. It offers an opportunity to connect with an audience and gain valuable experience that can advance your playing.

Fourth, you learn about how to continue your guitar journey. This is what's great about learning the guitar: the journey can continue as long as you'd like. There is always more to learn. Allowing you to continue exploring and growing in the process.

Lastly, to continue growing as a guitarist, consider private lessons, online courses, tutorials, or joining workshops and classes. All of these avenues can provide a more enjoyable learning experience and keep you engaged over time.

Acoustic Guitar Mastery: Conclusion

Congratulations on reaching the end of the "Beginner's Guide to Acoustic Guitar Mastery"! You've taken significant steps in developing your understanding and skills of the acoustic guitar and in building the confidence to do so.

Each chapter has provided you with the tools and knowledge necessary to grow as a guitarist. You've learned to appreciate the delicate nuances of tuning, mastered fundamental chords, scales, and experimented with a variety of playing techniques.

These foundational skills form the bedrock of your musical journey, enabling you to express yourself creatively and confidently. The acoustic guitar is more than just an instrument; it's a means of personal expression and a companion on your musical adventure.

By embracing the techniques and concepts outlined in this guide, you're not only developing technical proficiency but also discovering your unique musical voice.

Whether you're strumming a simple chord progression or crafting intricate melodies, remember that each note you play is a reflection of your personal style and passion for music.

As you continue to hone your skills, don't forget the importance of regular practice and goal setting. Establishing clear, achievable goals will keep you motivated and focused, ensuring steady progress and personal satisfaction.

Take time to reflect on how far you've come since you first picked up the acoustic guitar. Acknowledge the progress you've made, the challenges you've overcome, and the skills you've acquired. Reflecting on your journey helps you appreciate your achievements and sets the stage for future growth.

Lastly, never underestimate the power of community and collaboration. Engage with other musicians, share your experiences, and learn from one another. Whether through jam sessions, performances, or online forums, connecting with fellow guitarists can inspire and encourage you on your journey.

To all your success,

Sincerely, Dwayne Jenkins

Other Books From Dwayne Jenkins

Learn Guitar Scale Theory:

Dive deep into guitar scale theory with this easy to learn from, comprehensive guidebook. An understanding of theory can add a rich vocabulary for both harmony and melody.

Learning guitar scale theory will help you expand your improvisation skills, enhance your scale vocabulary, and deepen your understanding of intervals.

Learn to Play the Ukulele.

Another great instrument to learn to play is the ukulele. Very similar to the acoustic guitar, but with only four strings. A versatile instrument that will complement the acoustic.

With step-by-step instructions, diagrams, notation, and exercises. All that will be needed is your desire to learn and time to practice. Explore the fun of playing the ukulele.

Learn Guitar Chord Theory:

If you'd like to learn more about chord theory and enhance your knowledge of chord construction, this book will do it. A great way to expand your guitar chord vocabulary.

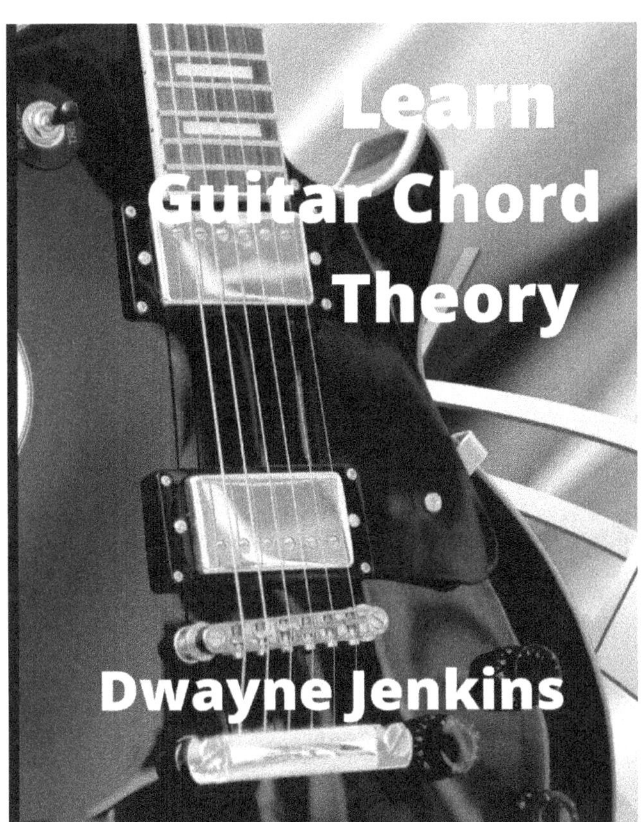

Learn Guitar Chord Theory is a comprehensive study guide on the inner workings of guitar chords, with step-by-step lessons, diagrams, exercises, and learning assessments. All designed to unlock the mysteries of the fretboard.

All books are authored by Dwayne Jenkins, published by Tritone Publishing, and are available worldwide.

Digital formats of all titles are available for instant learning. Just download them to your computer and start learning anywhere, anytime.

Self-study is a great way to learn, as it allows you not only to go at your own pace but also to develop self-discipline and time management, which can benefit you in other areas of your life.

Also, check out Dwayne's Guitar Lessons video channel on YouTube. These are free lessons covering a wide range of guitar topics.

Whether you are working on rhythm, lead, theory, or guitar maintenance, it is all here in these lessons. These are available 24 hours a day, 7 days a week, 365 days a year.

If more help is needed, Dwayne also offers one-on-one coaching on his website.

www.DwaynesGuitarLessons.com

Best of luck, and be sure to have fun.

About the Author

Dwayne Jenkins is a guitar teacher with a unique, engaging approach that helps students of all ages and skill levels enjoy playing the guitar and ukulele. His enthusiasm and love for teaching shine through every lesson that he creates.

His lessons are designed to help you progress. No matter your reason for learning, there will always be something in Dwayne's books and products to help you achieve your dreams.

So if you're a student looking to start or a student looking to further your education, be sure to get involved with Dwayne's guitar lessons and learn what so many people have already discovered: why learning to play the guitar is one of the most incredible things you can do for yourself.

What Students Are Saying About Dwayne's Guitar Lessons

"Dwayne, thank you so much for everything you have taught me and done for me. You are an amazing guitarist and wonderful teacher" B.I

"Dwayne, it has been a true pleasure to have you at our house each week! Ken & Trevor have learned so much through you and your teachings. Thank you!" Lisa.

"Dwayne, thank you for being a great teacher and teaching me many great songs. This is a skill that will last me a lifetime." Danielle.

"Dwayne, we want you to know we are honored to have you at the studio. We appreciate all that you do and are grateful that we can leave you in charge." Angie & Wilson M.E.C.

"Dwayne, we are so glad you are our Teacher. It's been three years already, can you believe it? Thank you again. You're the best!" Chelsey & Lucas.

"Dwayne, we are so glad that you are in our lives. Chelsey & Lucas enjoy their time with you and look up to you. Looking forward to another great year! Love and best wishes, Ken & Sue.

"Dwayne, thank you so much for being not only an awesome guitar teacher but an awesome friend as well," Kayla.

"Dwayne, thank you so much for all the years of doing lessons. You have been very patient with my progress, helped me build confidence, and inspired me to pursue my dreams. And in doing so, you have become a great friend." Jake.

"Dwayne, thank you for teaching Nick guitar so well. He loves it and is getting quite good, fast. I'm amazed!" Jane.

"Dwayne, thank you so much for teaching me every Saturday, and not only teaching me guitar but also about life, and helping me with setting my goals. You are a great teacher, mentor, and the best friend ever." Carson.

"There is no other person I would want to teach me a guitar! His 1-on-1 teaching makes learning guitar very personal & exhilarating. He teaches at your pace and takes pride in what YOU want to learn. The best part is that if Dwayne doesn't know a song a student wants to play, he takes time out of the week to learn it. His teaching comes to life in my performance and has progressed over the last 8 years. Words cannot describe how amazing a teacher, rockstar, and true friend Dwayne has become to me." Dominic.

Resource Guide

The Major and Minor Scales

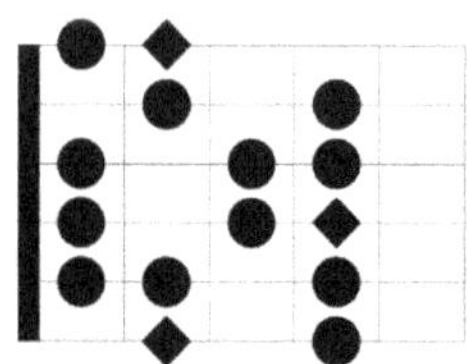

The Major Scale

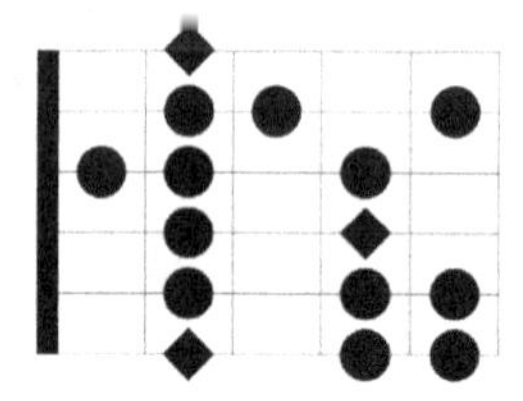

The Natural Minor

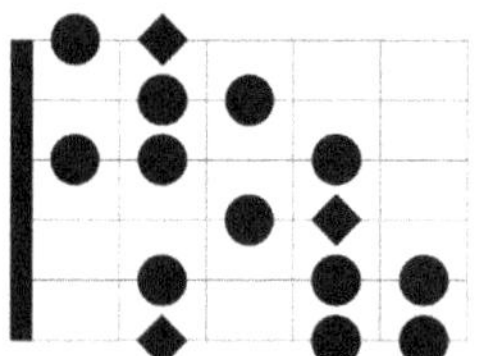

The Harmonic Minor

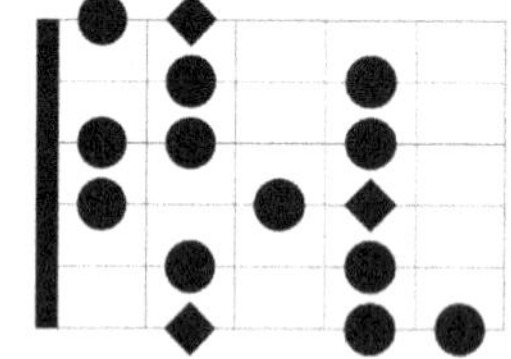

The Melodic Minor

The Major Scale: 1 2 3 4 5 6 7 Octave

The Natural Minor Scale: 1 2 b3 4 5 b6 b7 Octave

The Harmonic Minor Scale: 1 2 b3 4 5 b6 7 Octave

The Melodic Minor Scale: 1 2 b3 4 5 6 7 Octave

Each minor scale produces a different shade of color.

Resource Guide Continued

The Five Major Pentatonic Scales

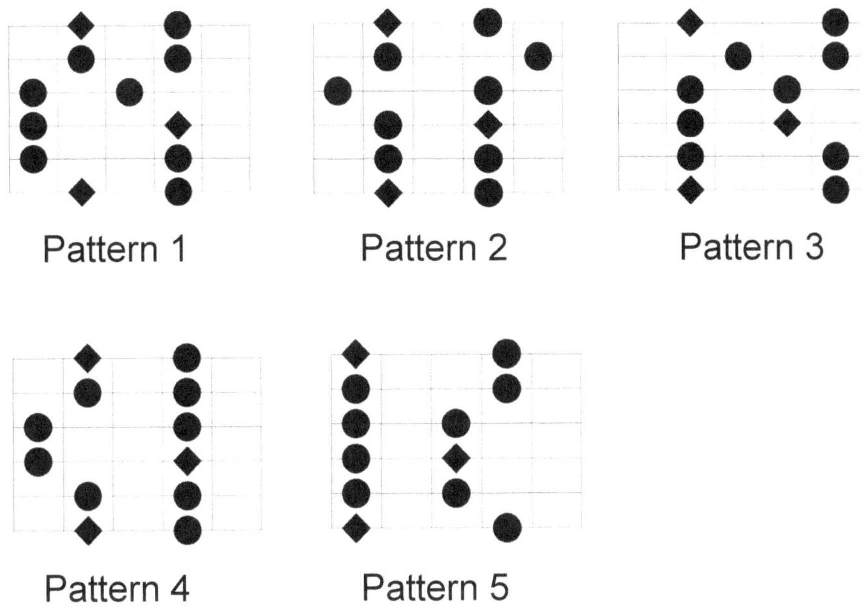

Pattern 1   Pattern 2   Pattern 3

Pattern 4   Pattern 5

Things to remember:

1. It is a five-note scale that produces a bright, happy sound.
2. The number value is 1 2 3 5 6.
3. Key Example, C Major: C D E G A
4. Created by eliminating the 4th and 7th notes of the major.
5. Each pattern starts on a tone degree of the scale.

Master all five scale patterns in both major and minor.

The Five Minor Pentatonic Scales

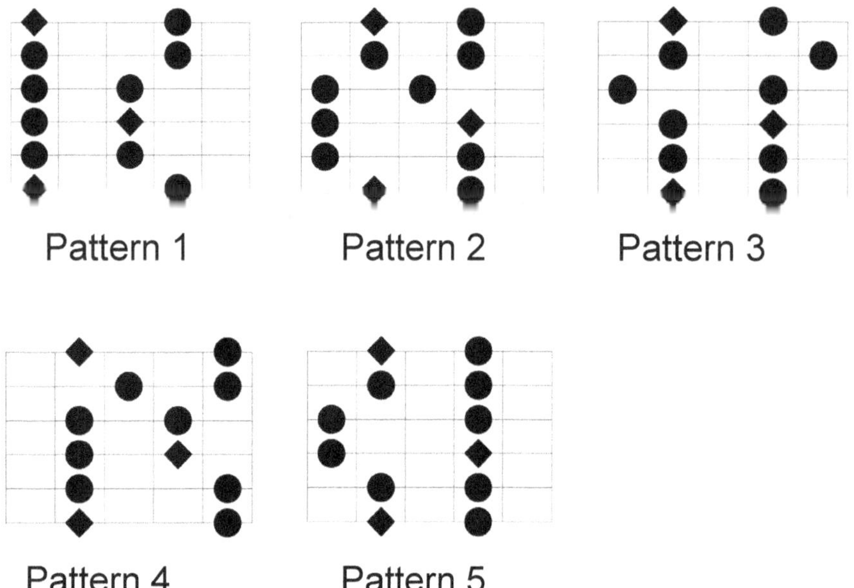

Pattern 1   Pattern 2   Pattern 3

Pattern 4   Pattern 5

1. It is a five-note scale that produces a sad, somber sound.
2. The number value is 1 b3 4 5 b7
3. Key example, A minor: A C D E G
4. Created by eliminating the 2nd and 6th of the major.
5. Each pattern starts on a tone degree of the scale.

These five-note scale patterns are essential for lead guitar mastery. Once you get these down, move on to mastering the blues scales and the modes.

Although simple, do not overlook their potency. Many great blues and rock guitarists use them.

Resource Guide Continued

Common chords

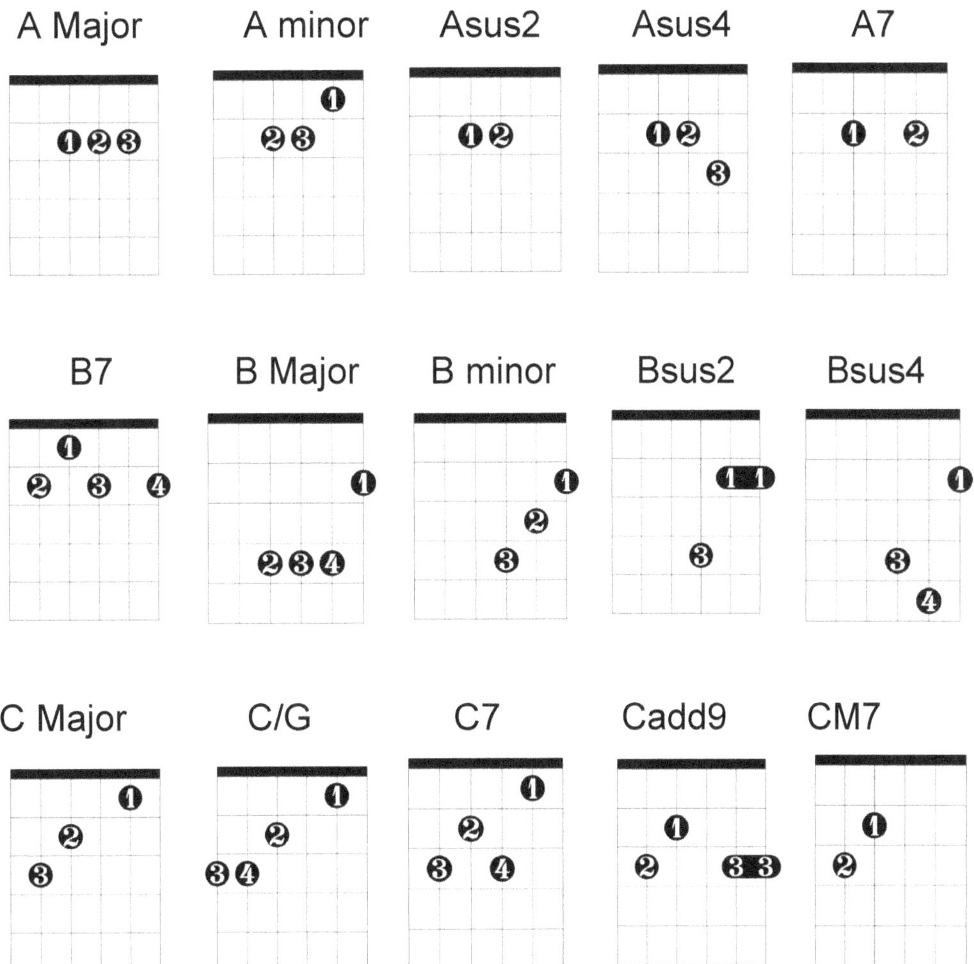

These are all chords found in many of your favorite songs.
Learn them and have them handy for when needed.

Resource Guide Continued

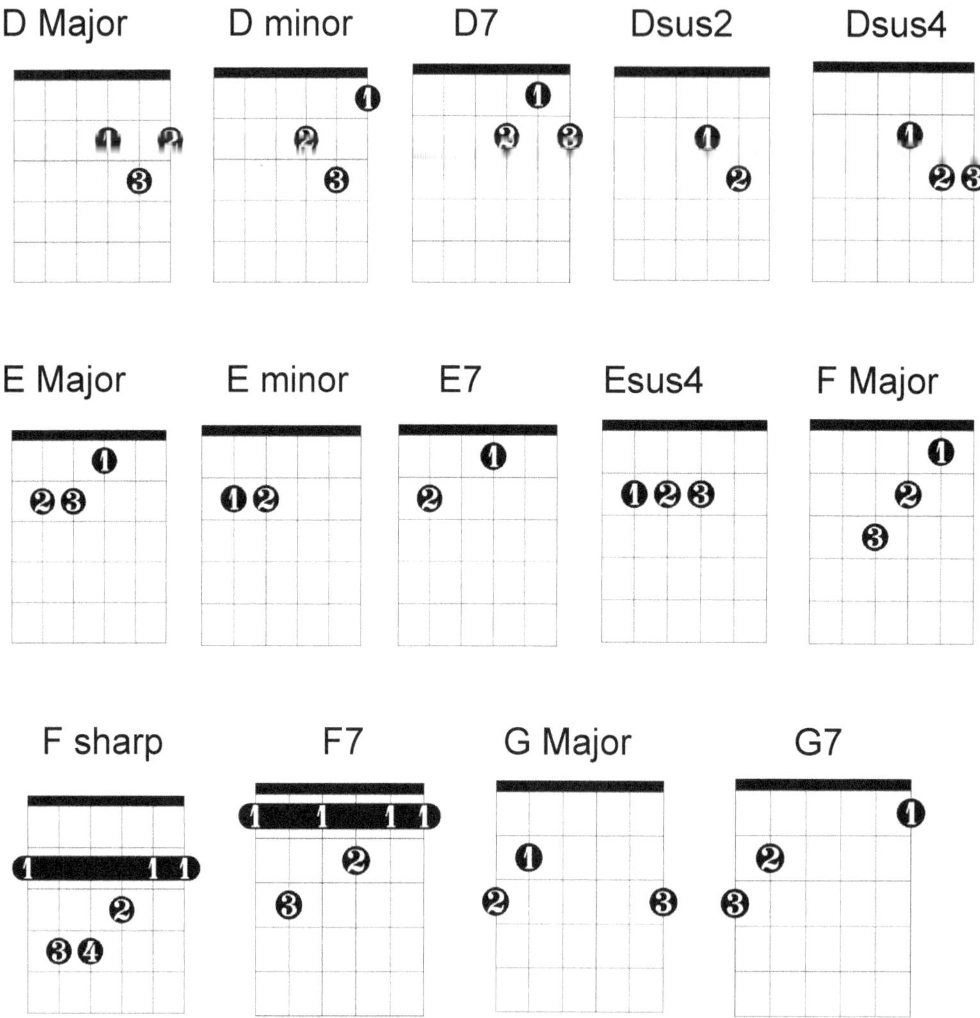

Remember, the F sharp and F7 are barre chords and are played with your index finger barring across all six strings. Not easy to start with, but very beneficial in the long run.

Resource Guide Continued

12-Bar Blues Progression: I-IV-V Key of G major = G C D

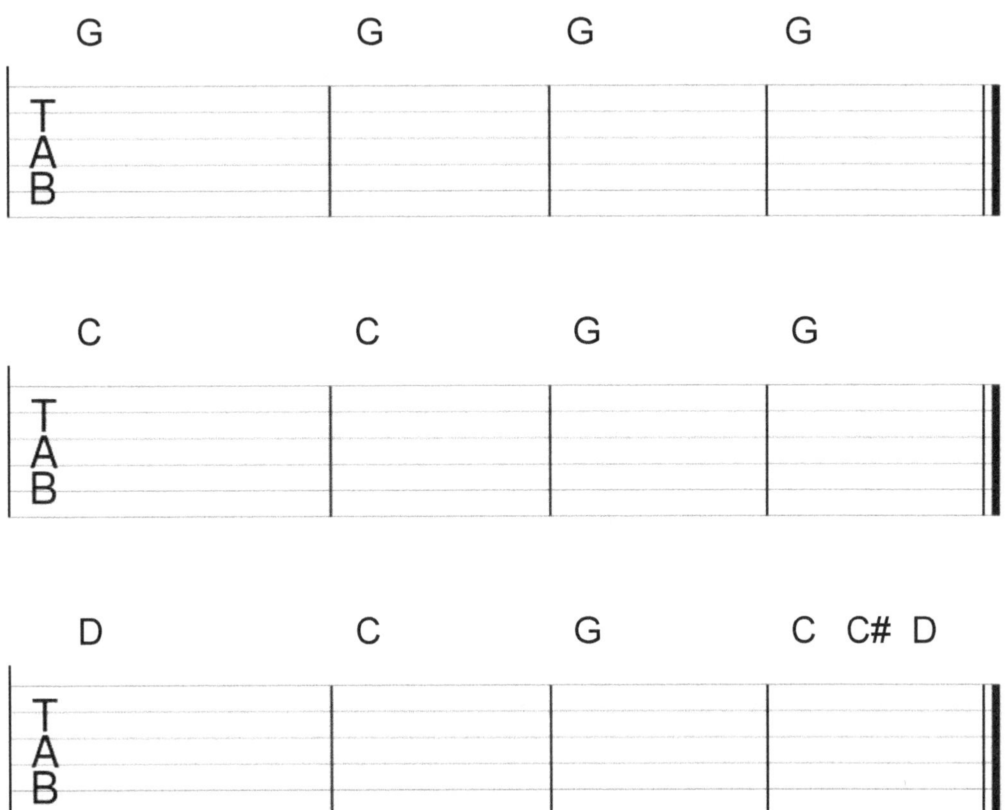

The last measure is what's called a turnaround. Utilizing the flat 5th chord. Common in the blues, and takes you back to the root chord to start all over.

Practice this progression in different keys with different chords, always using the 1st, 4th, and 5th chords of each key.

Resource Guide Continued

Notes Within Common Major Keys: W-W-H-W-W-W-H

1. A Major: A B C# D E F# G# octave
2. B major: B C# D# F F# G# A# octave
3. C Major: C D E F G A B octave
4. D Major: D E F# G A B C# octave
5. E Major: E F# G# A B C# D# octave
6. F Major: F G A Bb C D E octave
7. G Major: G A B C D E F# octave

Notes Within Common Minor Keys: W-H-W-W-H-W-W

1. A minor: A B C D E F G octave
2. B minor: B C# D E F# G A octave
3. C minor: C D Eb F G Ab Bb octave
4. D minor: A Bb C D E F G octave
5. E minor: E F# G A B C D octave
6. F minor: F G Ab Bb C Db Eb octave
7. G minor: G A Bb C D Eb F octave

Two Extra Common Minor Keys: W-H-W-W-H-W-W

1. B flat minor: Bb C Db Eb F Gb Ab
2. F sharp minor: F# G# A B C# D E

All the information in this resource guide has been covered in the training and presented here for easier reference. All scales presented are commonly found in many songs in many styles of music.

Chords covered in the training are presented, as well as others that are commonly found in many songs. Once you learn to read chord charts, I recommend you learn all the chords and add them to your vocabulary.

Notes within common keys are also presented to help you understand the inner workings of musical keys. You will encounter these in your playing, and they will help you better understand scale and chord construction.

The more chords and scales you have in your guitar playing arsenal, the better you'll be at figuring out songs and composing ones of your own. Making you a well-rounded musician.